# BOTHAM

## HERO AND VILLAIN

Compiled and edited by Alastair McLellan

TWO HEADS
PUBLISHING

First published in 1997 by
Two Heads Publishing
9 Whitehall Park
London N19 3TS

ISBN 1 897850 87 5

Cover photograph – Allsport
Cover design by Angelo Acanfora
Printed and bound in Great Britain by Biddles Limited

For Charles, Jim and the Inside Edge team

# CONTENTS

# INTRODUCTION

If you want to be the best, you have got to have tunnel vision. Things can only be black and white – no grey areas, because that is where doubt creeps in. And you can never look back. What happened yesterday is gone, finished. It is always today and tomorrow that counts. That is what I was like from the age of 14. Nothing else mattered.
*Ian Botham*

I've got to practice it. When I get older, people will want my autograph.
*A 10 year-old Ian Botham explains to his mother why he keeps signing his own name over and over*

Ian Botham has led a life more dramatic, more packed full of incident, both on and off the field, than any other cricketer, arguably more than any other British sportsman. In winning the 1981 Ashes series almost single-handedly he created one of British sport's most potent talismans. Botham is also, perhaps, the most controversial figure British sport has ever produced.

Ian Botham arrived in English cricket at a time when

many of the game's 'traditions' were coming under pressure. Kerry Packer showed that the world's cricket authorities could no longer take their control of the game for granted, media coverage of cricket was intensifying and concentrating more on the 'personality' of players and England's position as one of the world's top three sides was being threatened by the 'junior' Test playing nations.

English cricket needed a saviour, the media needed a star and the game's authorities needed someone to restore the popularity of the 'official' game. Ian Botham fitted the bill perfectly... but for only so long as he knew his place.

Soon the old cricketers who had enjoyed watching him wallop the Aussies started to complain that Botham was getting too big for his boots, the game's authorities grew alarmed at his increasingly exuberant 'social life' and the media became bored with praising him and decided that finding his faults would be more fun. His disastrous reign as England captain in 1980-1981 was enough to start the Botham backlash, big time. Despite the miracle of the 1981 Ashes series the bandwagon hasn't stopped rolling since.

And now Botham is back. The man who poured scorned on those who ran the English game during his days as a player, wants to become one of them. He is still the best known cricketer in the UK. Everyone, even those who have never watched a game of cricket in their lives, has an opinion on Ian Botham. His recent high profile libel case against former Pakistan captain Imran Khan has only served to heighten the debate over Botham's place in the English game and English society.

So. Ian Botham. The world's greatest all-rounder or an overweight chancer who got lucky? The man who saved English cricket or the man who betrayed it through poor fitness and questionable dedication? A patriot who enshrines all that's best about Britain or a loutish loudmouth whose prejudices reek of the 'little Englander'? A boisterous, likeable rogue or a bully? A dedicated and misunderstood family man or a play-boy? Hero or Villain? Or both?

This book presents Ian Botham's life in the way that he lived it – as a series of major and minor sporting and personal explosions. His greatest triumphs and disasters are described by those who were there and by the man himself. His impact on cricket, on sport and on Britain is revealed through the words of his team mates, opponents, friends, family and the game's leading observers. You'll also find that those with an opinion on Ian Botham range from Elton John to the broadsheet leader writers – stressing just how all-pervasive his influence on the British psyche has been during the last twenty years.

No other cricketer – and precious few sportsmen – has ever inspired such feelings of excitement, delight, anger and despair. It is those feelings, packed tighter than a West Indian slip cordon, which are contained between the covers of this book.

*Alastair McLellan*

# 1972-1979

## NO WONDER THEY CALLED
## YOU GOLDEN BALLS

IAN TERENCE BOTHAM WAS BORN ON THE 24TH NOVEMBER 1955 in Heswall, Cheshire. His father served in the Fleet Air Arm, before, eventually, coming to work for Westland Helicopters in Yeovil, Somerset, his wife and infant son in tow.

ITB began to display his sporting prowess almost as soon as he could walk and by 1972, at the age of 16, he was faced with having to decide between a career as a professional footballer or a first-class cricketer. He chose cricket and joined the MCC ground-staff  at Lord's – a traditional nursery for promising county cricketers. Cricket's greatest roller-coaster ride was about to begin.

## 1972-1973

He had all the attributes: ball skills, speed, timing and, above all, enthusiasm. We felt he was a pretty safe bet for the First Division.
*Crystal Palace manager Bert Head*

Match manager's reports and records of every player's performance are kept in the Cricket Office,

at the corner of the pavilion. In the files lie such fascinating details as the performance of IT Botham in his
first MCC match in 1972 against the Universities
Athletic Union. He made nought and took no wicket
for 23 runs.
*The Times on ITB's early days*

A very outstanding cricketer who shows a great deal
of promise but does everything in his own way. He
needs a lot of guidance and is proving better with the
bat than the ball, possibly because he has not had a
great deal of opportunity, although in the course of
time will prove to be a more than useful bowler.
*MCC coach Les Muncer*

Pisshole shot Botham, pisshole shot. But if you keep
hitting it son, you keep playing it.
*MCC coach Harry Sharp*

Botham lived with Rodney Ontong in a small flat,
where they made no effort whatsoever to live within
their means. They decided that they could not
possibly spread their wages far enough, and preferred
one good binge to blow it all away. After that they
cajoled and persuaded funds from friends. Ian was
not a great worrier in those days; tomorrow would
look after itself.
*Peter Roebuck*

After shrugging off a handful of lads, it took another
half-dozen to pin him down and apply the white-
wash. He got the highest marks in history for resist-

ing. He was just sixteen and some of the blokes he'd seen off were in their early twenties. A week later, there was a knock on the door of the senior dressing room and in walked Botham – that was taboo for a start. He asked if anyone fancied whitewashing him again.

*Jim Alldis, head boy on the Lord's ground staff*

Somerset, meanwhile, had been noting ITB's progress at Lord's and gave him an extended run in the county 2nd XI during 1973. Towards the end of the season they also decided he was ready for the big time.

Botham's [first team] debut [for Somerset] was against Lancashire. He announced himself by cracking three fierce boundaries before tamely offering a catch to short extra cover. He returned to the pavilion in a cloud of dust, storming into the dressing room to utter the oft-repeated words, 'I should have belted the ruddy thing harder'.

*Peter Roebuck*

## 1974

In 1974, at the age of just 18, ITB became a regular in Somerset's first team. Early in the season came a fateful clash with Hampshire in the Benson & Hedges Cup.

Now came a schoolboy's dream of a match-winning innings. Botham batted, unlike his seniors, with sensible aggression. He and Moseley added 63 for the ninth wicket, profiting from crafty running between

wickets. Suddenly, with seven overs remaining, Somerset were in with an outside chance. With 38 needed to win, Botham hooked a six, but was then hit in the mouth by a bouncer from Roberts. However, he was quick to take guard and with five overs left only 18 were required. Botham hooked another six, and Somerset were 7 runs short when Moseley was lbw to Roberts for 24. There were then 16 balls left with the last pair in. Botham contrived to keep the bowling but he played and missed three times in Herman's last over before striking the winning boundary.
*The Daily Telegraph*

BLOOD, SWEAT AND CHEERS FOR BOTHAM
Ian Botham, a young man of 18 from Yeovil, played not only the innings of his life when he made 45 not out, taking Somerset from 133 for eight to 184 for nine and victory by one wicket over Hampshire in the Benson and Hedges Cup, but he also lifted the game from a state of conventional excitement to one of unbelievable suspense and drama and finally into the realms of romantic fiction.
*Henry Blofeld in The Guardian*

As I look back on it, hitting me in the mouth was the worst thing Andy could have done. It seemed to relax me.
*ITB*

Ian was bowling little medium-pace 'dobbers', but he could already swing it, coming in all jaunty off about fifteen paces and with a good sideways-on-action.

Within two or three years, of course, he'd put on
weight and three or four yards of pace and was
running in fully intent on some fireball-quick mischief
– and English cricket was never quite the same again.
*Graham Gooch remembers his first encounter*

In a Benson and Hedges match Botham bowled Barry
Richards with an ill-disciplined delivery. Richards,
shocked at his fall to this intemperate youth, turned to
Derek Taylor to accuse him of kicking over the stumps
from behind.
*Peter Roebuck*

Brian Close's on-the-field rows with Ian Botham fairly
shook the ground from time to time, orchestrated by
much gesticulating, yet both men retain an abiding
affection for each other. Possibly they are two of a
kind: strong, aggressive, irrational, but loyal, honest
and popular.
*Peter Roebuck on ITB's relationship with his first county
captain*

He gave me the killer instinct.
*ITB on Brian Close*

He was quiet and nice and he helped me find my car
in the rain.
*Kathy Waller (soon to be Botham) meets ITB*

## 1975

One minute he would look a big whacker of the ball,
not very cultured and the next he would play this

mature, controlled shot. I didn't know what to make
of him.
*Mike Brearley's first meeting with ITB*

In those days, we didn't have much money and Both
would take bets that he could drink three pints of beer
in under a minute. It was worse than robbing a bank.
*ITB's flat mate Dennis Breakwell*

To tell you the truth, seeing this scruffy looking place,
I wouldn't sell anything to you anyway.
*Drumstick salesman ITB gets shirty with a reluctant shop
owner*

If Ian does anything to hurt Kathy, I'll kill him, and if
Kathy stands in the way of Ian's career, I'll give her a
roasting as never was.
*Brian Close on ITB and Kathy's wedding*

## 1976

Botham is a fine striker and timer of the ball with a
full, clean, flowing stroke of the bat and – almost a
'must' in present-day cricket – he is not frightened to
hit the ball. His 167 not out at Trent Bridge was an
innings almost out of the Vivian Richards mould – it
won us the match against the clock and was worth
going miles to see. Botham's youthful impetuosity
and confidence gets him out on occasions when he is
well set, but experience and time will teach him to
temper his aggression with a little patience: an exciting prospect for the future.
*Brian Close*

Hours after ensconcing himself in my home he received a phone message from his wife Kathryn: she was pregnant with their first child. Not for a moment was there a hint of regret at being absent from home at such an auspicious time. Fortune had brought Botham here, and now he was innocently and hugely delighted at yet another treasure that life had thrown up on the shore of his experience.

*Former England fast bowler Frank Tyson, with whom ITB stayed during the winter of 1976-77 while in Australia on the Whitbread scholarship*

## TEST DEBUT V AUSTRALIA 1977

After three years on the county circuit, the only taste of international cricket that ITB had experienced was a couple of one-day internationals against the West Indies at the end of the 1976 season. In the middle of the 1977 season this changed when he was selected for the Third Ashes Test at Trent Bridge. ITB was about to introduce himself to the Australians.

Several people and places claim a share in Botham. There is Cheshire where he was born in 1955. There is Lord's where he spent two years on the staff. There is Bill Andrews ('spotted him at once, natural genius'). There is Yeovil, where he lives and where his interest in the game developed. Down in Somerset they have been saying for some time that he is the best all-rounder they have had since Arthur Wellard.

*Alan Gibson*

Did you hear the news? Chris Old has been declared
unfit. I bet you £5 you're picked to replace him.
*ITB's Somerset team-mate Dennis Breakwell (ITB accepted
and lost the bet)*

We looked on Botham not so much with disrespect, as
without respect.
*Aussie captain Greg Chappell on ITB's Test debut*

A bloody awful ball.
*ITB on his first Test wicket, Greg Chappell played on*

It looks like you have been doing some work.
*The Queen to ITB as she visited Trent Bridge after he had
taken five wickets in the Australian's first innings*

Botham was watched by his wife Kathryn, who is
eight months pregnant. He said: 'I just hope she is still
eight months pregnant after all this excitement'.
*The Sun*

## TO PAKISTAN AND NEW ZEALAND 1977-78

ITB played in two Tests against the Aussies in 1977,
missing the Fifth Test at The Oval through injury. At the
end of the season he was selected for his first Test tour.

He tried to take on the local leg-spinners and he was
hopeless.
*England captain Mike Brearley on why ITB did not feature
in any of the winter's three Tests against Pakistan*

I'm convinced Brearley stopped me playing in

Pakistan. He wanted to dominate everything and he was disturbed that this loudmouth from Somerset didn't gaze at him as if he was Moses.
*ITB*

My caddy, who was betting on me against Kenny Barrington's caddy, found my ball sitting up in the middle of the fairway. He told me to give it all I had: there was no way I could reach the green, which was over a hill and out of sight. I had a feeling I could reach the green, so I took a 2-wood and hit a screamer, right up the middle. I said, 'Ah, that's got to be close' and my caddy went white. When we reached the top of the hill, there was this great big pond in front of the green. It had a notice saying: 'Snake Infested Water – Do not send in your caddy'. By which time I was furious, and pretty soon I had the guy by the scruff of the neck and was yelling: 'You get in there and get that ball'. He went in. After that he had a lot more respect for my distance in hitting a ball.
*ITB kills time (and nearly his caddy) in Pakistan*

We have a complete mad man out here.
*Phil Edmonds phones his wife Frances during the tour*

When England arrived in New Zealand, ITB was included in the Test team. After a quiet game in the First Test, which England lost, ITB caused a sensation in the Second Test, in more ways than one.

No matter how long he plays for England, Botham will find it hard to equal his spectacular all-round

performance. His maiden Test century, in only his fourth game for England, included one 6 and twelve 4s, and was full of impressive and powerful strokes. In the second innings, when England led by 183 runs and quick runs were needed to ram home their advantage, Botham hit 30 off 36 balls. His bowling was equally convincing, with figures of five for 73 and three for 38, and he took three catches, two of which were in the sensational class.
*Wisden Cricketers' Almanack 1979*

Run him out, or you won't play again on this tour.
*Vice-captain Bob Willis' tells ITB to run-out the stand-in English captain because he was batting too slowly in the second innings*

I can't do that. He's the captain of England. He's Geoffrey Boycott.
*ITB's reply*

'What have you done? What have you done?' – 'I've run you out, you c***!'
*Exchange between ITB and Geoff Boycott after ITB had done as he was told*

## 1978

Back in England, ITB was now arguably the most important member of England's Test team after less than a year in international cricket. At Lord's he furthered his one-man mission to rewrite the record books by scoring 108 and taking 8-34 against the visiting Pakistanis.

He walked though the door and made a bee-line for the corner and the sofa under the window. That was his place and that was the end of it.
*Lord's dressing room attendant Roy Harrington on ITB's first Test at HQ*

The fall of Pakistan's last eight wickets for 43 runs this morning, seven of them to Ian Botham, and the loss of the Second Test by an innings and 120 runs, looks miserable on paper, but the tourists were up against something out of the ordinary. For no obvious meteorological reason, on a cloudless morning, the ball swung prodigiously and Botham, in an astonishing piece of bowling, beat the bat with three or four outswingers an over.
*Michael Melford in the Daily Telegraph*

There was a great rip as I got the ball away.
*ITB describes the moment when his trousers tore during his century in the Lord's Test*

I don't see how you can serve two masters. Who in hell wants to play for a meaningless World XI where national pride doesn't come into it?
*ITB's rejects suggestions that he might join Kerry Packer's World Series*

I just wouldn't feel right. In any case my head is the hardest part of me.
*ITB on his decision not to wear a helmet*

## TO AUSTRALIA AND NEW ZEALAND 1978-79

Bill O'Reilly wrote in a local newspaper that he didn't think this chap Botham would give Australia much trouble in the series. That was all Ian needed. He took the new ball, finished with five wickets, in a ten-wicket victory and bowled especially well against their best batsman, Peter Toohey. A vote of thanks to Mr O'Reilly.

*Geoff Boycott on ITB's return against Aussie state side New South Wales after a month-long lay off for injury*

I hope Mike Brearley bought Ian Botham a large beer last night before his aching feet dragged him up to bed. For throughout the first day of the First Test against Australia, the Somerset giant with the Charles Atlas shoulders had borne the weight of Brearley's reputation as the shrewdest skipper since Captain Marvel. Because, and make no mistake, Brearley's decision to put Australia in on a perfect pitch on a perfect day put him one place below Maverick in the Who's Who of gamblers. That it succeeded – Australia were 232-8 at the close – owed more to Botham than stark figures can show.

*The Sun (ITB took 4-67 from 31 overs on the first day)*

Botham impressed me with his confidence in exercising authority. He responded with self-assured good humour to Boycott's jibes about his stripes needing a polish. It was Botham who was perceptive and confident enough to point out that in trying to deal with the extra bounce of Australian pitches

Boycott was becoming rooted to the back foot.
Botham's advice was, I think, crucial to Boycott at that
moment.
*Mike Brearley*

This man is a giant. Test grounds are becoming too
small for him. One day he may demolish an entire
grandstand with either bat or ball.
*The Daily Star*

That's that, now give me another.
*ITB's response to a Hadlee bouncer (which he'd hooked for
four)*

Both was highly amused when he was hit on the
head, he tapped his helmet and laughed heartily.
*David Gower remembers how ITB dealt with Aussie fast
bowler Rodney Hogg*

No wonder they call you Golden Bollocks.
*Mike Hendrick after ITB dismissed Kim Hughes at
Melbourne with another long hop*

Botham's tail was up and the fact that the yobs in the
crowd were having a go only made him more combat-
ive. They went mad as he walked back towards them,
yelling and swearing, a forest of V signs, and Botham
grinned and nodded as though they were on his side.
*Geoff Boycott on ITB in Melbourne*

Some Australians are like their country, big and
empty.
*ITB*

The man I would have liked in the Australian side was Ian Botham. We were short of an all-rounder who could take an attack by the scruff of the neck and swing a game, and who could also open with the new ball and field in any position with brilliance. With Botham in our side for the summer I fancy the series could have finished in our favour.
*Australian captain Graham Yallop speaking after his side's 5-1 defeat in the Test Series*

First the convicts, then the rabbits and now Botham.
*Banner held up by Australian spectators during the Test series*

More than anything it made me feel proud because I am a very patriotic person – and I felt that we achieved something for England. Like any touring side, we took a lot of stick at times from the Aussies – and it felt good to ram it all back down their throats.
*ITB on the Ashes victory*

## 1979

England were 58 for 4 by mid-morning of the first day. Botham came in but a proper contest was prevented by further rain that held up play for the next three days. Botham resumed on Monday and played one of his amazing innings. He had been 9 on Thursday afternoon, he was 108 with four balls to go before lunch on Monday. But evidently he did not realise that a single would have meant a century before lunch and he blocked the four balls.
*Mihir Bose on ITB's 137 at Headingley v India*

One of the finest innings I've seen in the last 20 years.
*TV commentator and former England Test star Jim Laker on ITB's century*

Ted Dexter was the last Englishman to hit so well; indeed it is hard to think that Jessop or anyone else ever hit a ball better than Botham did here.
*John Woodcock on the same innings*

Ian had a bad game at Taunton the other day and he came home and kicked the door in.
*Kathy Botham explains damage to the Bothams' Weston-Super-Mare home to a visitor*

## TO AUSTRALIA AND INDIA 1979-80

Once Richards had taunted him there was no way I was going to dissuade Botham from attacking the spinners, even if I wanted to, because if there is one thing Botham seeks, it is Viv's admiration and praise.
*Mike Brearley on ITB's demise in a World Series game*

Ian respected Mike and was even, in some ways, in awe of him. If Ian began horsing around at inappropriate times, Mike could put him down crushingly and Ian would immediately be as good as gold like an admonished schoolboy. No malice either given or taken, though. It was good to be in the same room when Brearley and Botham were rubbing sparks off each other, but Brearley's always were, in the end, the brightest.
*Graham Gooch*

But my jubilation was quickly flattened as I experienced the Gorilla Hug for the first time. It came of course from Ian Botham who traditionally greets the taker of any wicket for England by grabbing the poor fellow around the chest and squeezing the air from his lungs. It's nice to be appreciated by one's colleague but it does not do the health any good.
*Graham Dilley*

Ian got the whole team to pin me down and he stripped me naked. I had only my socks on. He then sprayed blobs of shaving foam over me; one on my nose, one each on my nipples, even one on my willy.
*Geoff Boycott*

England's 10-wicket victory over India in the Golden Jubilee Test with a day and a half to spare confirmed the frailty of much of England's batting and the uncomfortable extent to which the batting and, still more, the bowling is currently relying on the strength and all-round talents of Ian Botham.
*Michael Melford in the Daily Telegraph*

A giant of a cricketer.
*Mike Brearley on ITB after the match in which he had taken 13 wickets and scored 114*

From what I have seen on this tour Botham could be the next England captain. I think he has only one real opponent for the job – Middlesex all-rounder Phil Edmonds.
*John Edrich*

You'll have the most miserable time of your life.
*Brian Close warns ITB against accepting the England
captain's job if it is offered to him*

Once every year Ian Botham repairs to Scotland. He
descends upon Callandar, a village hidden in the
remote mountains north of Stirling. Ostensibly
Botham arrives for a holiday, a rest from his strenuous
lifestyle. The Scots, a hardy, resolute race, spend the
51 weeks between Ian's visits recovering their
strength, preparing their stamina for next April.
*Peter Roebuck*

With the triumphant performance in the Golden Jubilee
test against India, the first episode in ITB's cricketing
career came to a close. Ahead of him lay the new
challenges of coping with captaincy, declining fitness
and the attentions of the tabloid press. But, at the start
of the 1980s, he could look back on the most dramatic
and successful first three years ever experienced by a
Test cricketer.

## TEST RECORD: 1977-1979

| M | Inns | NO | Runs | HS | Av | 100s | 50s | Ct |
|---|---|---|---|---|---|---|---|---|
| 23 | 35 | 2 | 1336 | 137 | 40.48 | 6 | 3 | 36 |

| Ovs | Runs | W | Av | Best | 5w | 10w | SR |
|---|---|---|---|---|---|---|---|
| 1038 | 2575 | 139 | 18.52 | 8-34 | 14 | 3 | 44.81 |

# 1980-1981

## THE COMEBACK KID
### Ashes 1981

Headingley, the Third Test
Edgbaston, the Fourth Test
Old Trafford, The Fifth Test
Reflections on Botham's Ashes

ITB BEGAN THE 1980S WITH HIS STATUS AS ONE OF THE world's greatest all-rounders already assured. Ahead of him lay his next challenge, the captaincy of his country. The next two years were to prove the most eventful in a cricket career which was already defying belief.

Captaincy appeared to destroy his form but it returned with awesome power once he was stripped of his rank, after just over a year in the officers mess.

ITB's record during these two years was far from negligible, but it did show the first signs of the Botham magic beginning to fray at the edges.

## TEST RECORD: 1980-1981

| M | Inns | NO | Runs | HS | Av | 100s | 50s | Ct |
|---|------|----|------|----|-----|------|-----|-----|
| 16 | 29 | 1 | 641 | 149 | 22.89 | 2 | 2 | 19 |

| Ovs | Runs | W | Av | Best | 5w | 10w | SR |
|-----|------|---|-----|------|----|-----|-----|
| 580.2 | 1709 | 63 | 27.13 | 6-95 | 3 | 1 | 55.27 |

## 1980

Mike Brearley had announced his intention not to tour

with England in the future. The West Indies, unofficial World Test champions, were England's summer opponents. It was time for a change at the top of English cricket.

Soon England will be looking for someone to succeed Mike Brearley as captain. It was significant that, on the latest tour to Australia, Botham became one of the team selectors and might well get the England captaincy. It is argued that he lacks experience of leadership, but I remember Sir Leonard Hutton and Peter May playing under NWD Yardley and Stuart Surridge respectively. In fact, Hutton was never officially Yorkshire captain.
*Notes by the Editor, Wisden Cricketers' Almanack 1980*

Are we asking too much of Botham, with such heavy responsibilities as he already has? This was an argument used against Hutton and it is true that, by his last season, Australia 1954-55, the strain had told upon his batting. There is a real risk that Botham might burn himself up too soon, especially because of an exceptionally demanding and absurdly crowded Test programme in the next couple of years.
*Alan Gibson*

Botham has the support of everyone concerned with English cricket. The players will have to be 100 per cent behind him and if any of them aren't, they will not play for England.
*Chairman of selectors Alec Bedser announces ITB's appointment as captain*

We think Botham will succeed, but if doesn't, he'll have to knuckle down and play under someone else.
*Alec Bedser later in the same press conference*

Selectors are always being accused of not giving youngsters their chance, always waiting until it's too late. So we decided, because of all his potential, to see how he goes on.
*Alec Bedser continues*

Come on, do it for England, do it for me, just do it.
*ITB thumps Vic Marks on the chest and exhorts him to greater efforts during a One-day International against the West Indies*

My spot in the Lord's dressing room was an old leather sofa, in a corner but with a view of the game. I'm told that some great players adopted that sofa before me, but now it has been replaced by some modern furniture. I hope that does not signal a change of luck.
*ITB nominates Lord's as his favourite ground. His next three Tests at Lord's produced eight runs for four times out and seven wickets at 51.14*

After the Test series against the Windies, which England lost 1-0, ITB led England in the Centenary Test v Australia at Lord's.

On the third day, early morning rain had affected old pitches on the Tavern End of the square, the umpires, after several inspections, not judging the conditions fit

until a quarter to four. They became arbiters in the matter once Greg Chappell and Ian Botham, the respective captains, disagreed. The former whose side were batting and in the stronger position, was keen to play, Botham not so.
*EW Swanton*

MCC members were involved in a momentary scuffle with umpire Constant as the the umpires and captains moved into the Long Room after their fifth pitch inspection of the day. Ian Botham, the England captain, and Greg Chappell, his Australian counterpart, saw to it that matters got no worse.
*Wisden Cricketers' Almanack 1981*

It was the sort of behaviour one expects from football hooligans. I was walking out to make the final inspection with Chappell and the two umpires when I was hit on the back of the head by a hand. I did nothing about it, but as we were all walking in a man in his twenties grabbed the umpire David Constant by the tie and shoved and jostled him. Greg Chappell and I moved in to break it up.
*ITB*

The irony is that on the occasion of the disgraceful scene in the Lord's Pavilion, the honour of cricket should have been defended by an Australian captain whose great tactical contribution to the game was to instruct one of his bowlers to roll the ball along the ground, and an England captain one day to be suspended for bringing the game into disrepute.
*Benny Green*

On Tuesday I watched Procter play Botham at single wicket. Procter was out seven times, but after 70 had been deducted, scored 112. Botham was out nine times, and finished 27 runs behind.
*Alan Gibson*

If Steele was batting in my garden, I'd have to get up and close the curtains.
*ITB on Leicestershire's John Steel, who had a reputation as a stonewaller*

Sunny is terrified of dogs. Petrified in fact. If one appears on the field during a Gavaskar innings his composure is shattered. Needless to say Ian Botham misses no opportunity to invite dogs into our dressing room or, if he can't find a dog, Ian will offer a few hidden woofs of his own.
*Peter Roebuck on the travails of Sunil Gavaskar, who played for Somerset during the 1980 season*

## 1981

ITB's record as England captain of played six, lost one, drawn five would have satisfied many later in the decade, especially as his opponents had been the two best sides in the world. Despite this, ITB's position was fiercely debated in the press as he led the England team to the Caribbean for the return series against Clive Lloyd's Windies.

Let there be no doubt about it, Botham will be baited in the Caribbean and, unless he swims past the bait, England may lose her greatest cricketer of a generation.

*Dudley Doust on how an impending court case for assaulting sailor Steven Isbister would affect ITB*

Ian Botham always gets the benefit of my help – though I haven't known him bother asking much.
*Geoff Boycott at the pre-tour press conference*

What a twit.
*ITB on reading Boycott's comments in the press*

There's no way at all we should lose. If we do, then a few heads will roll. You could bat for ten days on this pitch and not get a result.
*ITB before the first test (England scored 178 and 169 and lost by an innings and 79 runs)*

Only twelve months ago Botham found taking Test wickets as easy a pastime as doing the *Sun* crossword: he could experiment in the Test arena as though he was larking around in the nets. Now you could almost sense Greenidge and Haynes sneering as they dismissed his trundlers from their presence.
*Frank Keating*

Okay, okay, I know it was a stupid shot. Sure, I might not have tried it except it was Vivvy bowling.
*ITB after holing out to Viv Richards*

Fetch that.
*ITB to Joel Garner after hitting him for four*

I'm sorry, I can't play against that sort of thing.
*ITB after being dismissed a few overs later*

Every 'phone that I am talking to you on is listened to.
*ITB during Robin Jackman's deportation from Guyana*

It's like being smashed on the chest by a mallet.
*ITB's reaction to the death of friend and assistant tour
manager Ken Barrington*

The spirit of the side was quite good, but even though
we had a very professional core of players – Willey,
Gooch, Emburey, Boycott – it was a bit chaotic under
Botham. He surrounded himself with his drinking
mates, Graham Stevenson, and one or two others, and
we didn't really see much of him.
*Paul Downton*

When he was a member of the team and done one or
two pranks, you could tell him to get stuffed. But it's
a bit different when he's captain.
*Geoff Boycott*

I think the media must write that whenever it's
raining.
*ITB hits out at suggestions that he should stand down as
captain*

There has been heartwarming laughter and friendship
between the sides in this series, for which Botham
deserves far and away the most credit.
*Frank Keating*

Botham was given the captain's job too early. Looking
back, the decision seems more monstrous than it did
at the time, like lobbing a hand grenade, with the pin

long out, into the hands of the most promising recruit. Botham was given the job in circumstances that demanded that he also be given a chance. As a chance, two consecutive series against the West Indies is that of a snowball in hell.
*Robin Marlar*

When I was first given the captain's job I said it would be two years before I could get to grips with it.
*ITB*

Frustrated by his inability to defy single-handedly the fierce West Indian pace attack, his cricket became self-conscious. His cricket was inhibited and his personality too tense to relax.
*Peter Roebuck*

I thought they were friends of mine.
*ITB reacts to press criticism of his captaincy*

I think Brearley should have been used to give Ian Botham much needed experience before Botham took over the England captaincy. As a good player of fast bowling and a first-rate tactician, Brearley would have held his own against the West Indian quickies in England, while Botham leant his trade as vice captain without the full glare of press interest on him. It would have been easier for Botham first time round in the Caribbean: there the English press would have banded together, killed all those boring stories about the Botham waistline and supported him. In a wet English summer, when there's no cricket to write

about, Fleet Street will seize a topic and never let it go. In the 1980 English season that topic was Botham, his form and his weight – they even asked his wife what she cooks for him. If Brearley had still been skipper, Botham would have fared better. After all, he's got the job for as long as he wants, because there's no one else who is a certainty to play for England for the next five years.
*Mike Procter*

ITB returned from the tour of the West Indies, which had seen England lose the series 3-0, a much chastened man. Ahead of him lay a six match series against Australia. Even the wildest romantics among the cricket press could not imagine what the next few months would bring.

I think I'm improving all the time as a captain and I'm starting to get in better order with the bat.
*ITB after losing the First Test*

Botham is not the player he was. He may not be seen for two seasons at the top level. His from does not warrant a place in the England team.
*Ray Illingworth*

Talk of Botham being dropped was a great fillip to us.
*Dennis Lillee*

Lillee said, 'why don't you just give it away'.
*ITB on what the great Australian bowler told him when he complained about the pressures of captaincy*

Botham did not fit my idea of an England captain, whom I felt should have been a lot older than his twenty-four years and also with a lot more experience as a county captain.
*Graham Dilley*

One of the most ludicrous decisions ever made by the selectors in the history of English cricket.
*ITB (in 1995) on the selectors' decision to appoint him as captain on a match-by-match basis during the Ashes series*

I'm afraid that's not just good enough.
*BBC TV commentator Tony Lewis as ITB is dismissed for a pair in the Second Test at Lord's*

I walked back. The Long Room was incredibly, awesomely silent. No one said a thing. It was a bitter moment, as if I were being shut out.
*ITB describes the reaction of MCC members*

I ignored them then and I ignored them for a long time after.
*ITB speaking about the MCC members, in 1995*

It was one of the most embarrassing moments – the crowd felt embarrassed for him – that I've ever experienced.
*Christopher Martin-Jenkins*

Basically I feel that it's unfair to myself and the team to continue on a match-by-match basis. I don't what's happening and the team doesn't know what's happening.

*ITB explains his decision to 'resign' the captaincy*

The press asked me a direct question – 'Were we going to replace Ian Botham?' and I said yes, but that he had said he'd like it to be said that he'd resigned.
*Alec Bedser*

If you signed the c***, you can sack the c***.
*Sun Editor Kelvin McKenzie tells his sport editor to dispense with ITB's services as a columnist after he loses the captaincy*

The initial mistake was to make him captain in the first place. He hadn't sowed his wild oats. He wasn't a mature enough personality to take the job on at that stage.
*Christopher Martin-Jenkins*

He was never so at ease with the world again, for he had been let down by the people he believed in and he felt terribly alone.
*Peter Roebuck on ITB losing the captaincy*

I fear that Botham will never reproduce his brilliant displays in Test cricket. The truth is he was playing above himself and he will never be the same force again.
*Greg Chappell after the Lord's Test*

Within hours of making that decision Ian looked a lot more relaxed. At that moment I felt he was a man with a mission.
*Viv Richards*

## HEADINGLEY, THE THIRD TEST

If you think I've been poleaxed, hung drawn and quartered, if you leave me out of this Test match, you'll find out what it really means.
*ITB's reaction to Brearley's suggestion that he should sit out the Headingley Test (as remembered by Mike Gatting)*

A wonderful sight to see him hitting the ball with the same old freedom. It really looks like the shackles have dropped from his shoulders.
*Christopher Martin-Jenkins on ITB's first innings 50*

A lot of us, the senior players in the side, were thinking on the rest day that this was our last Test match.
*Bob Willis remembers how he felt with England staring defeat in the face*

In most people's minds, that game was already lost.
*David Gower*

Cricket's hierarchy would probably pass out with shock if they knew how much booze was put away by certain England players and myself between the Saturday night and the Monday when I hit my unbeaten 149 in the amazing Headingley Ashes Test.
*ITB (speaking in 1995)*

It was in the days when Sunday was always a rest day. England looked dead and buried on the Saturday and everyone was a bit down. Nowadays there would be a team meeting and extra nets, but what did we do on the Saturday night? Went on the beer. And it didn't

stop until well into Sunday. There was me, Botham, Graham Dilley, Bob Willis and a few others. It's all a bit of a blur really. We downed pint after pint and most of us could not even remember where we flaked out.
*Wayne Larkins (also speaking in 1995) remembers the same incident*

Just before we were going out, I thought 'this is stupid, funny things happen in cricket'.
*Dennis Lillee on his decision to put a bet on England to win the match, at odds of 100-1. He won £7,500*

What a triumph it would be for him, if he could still be batting at 6 O'clock this evening.
*Christopher Martin-Jenkins, commentating as ITB comes to the wicket*

Alderman, pitching the ball up, inviting him to drive...and Botham needs no second invitation.
*Christopher Martin-Jenkins commentates as ITB clubs Alderman to the long-off boundary*

There's no point looking for that, let alone chasing it. It's gone straight into the confectionery stand and out again.
*Richie Benaud, as ITB hits for six*

He has become a national hero once again.
*Christopher Martin-Jenkins as ITB leaves the field with 145 not out*

England were 135 for seven, still 92 behind, and the

distant objective of avoiding an innings defeat surely their only available prize. The England players' decision to check out of their hotel seemed a sound move. Three hours later, the registration desks around Leeds were coping with a flood of re-bookings, Botham having destroyed the game's apparent set course with an astonishing, unbeaten 145.
*Wisden Cricketers' Almanack 1982*

Botham's innings contained strokes that were classical, rugged and improvised, not all off the middle of the bat but hit with a power that forced seven Australian fielders to the boundary.
*Michael Melford in the Daily Telegraph*

It was Botham who stopped the rot at Headingley with an innings of such astonishing aggression it must be wondered who he was actually thrashing. Could it be that Ian had Alec Bedser in his sights.
*Allen Synge*

The players trooped from the field with England 124 in front and Botham 145. Bob Taylor popped into the visitors' dressing room and was told to go forth and multiply. He reported back that the tourists were a beaten side. In three hours of carnage the mood of a team, a game, a series and even a country had changed.
*Peter Roebuck*

It's all over and it's one of the most fantastic victories ever known in Test match history.

*Richie Benaud, as Willis takes the last Australian wicket and England win by 18 runs*

*Peter West:* Ian, you said if we can get another 50, that would make it interesting. You got another four.
*ITB:* Well, that made it even more interesting.
*Post match-interview*

The amazing Ian Botham had the mourners dancing in the aisles at Headingley last night with the greatest comeback since Lazarus.
*The Daily Express*

A captain's performance that came one match too late.
*Fred Trueman awards the man of the match award to ITB*

He hadn't used it much during the match and I thought there were a few runs left in it.
*ITB on his decision to use Graham Gooch's bat for the Headingley innings (Gooch had scored 2 and 0)*

All the time Botham helped me to relax with his presence at the other end. If I played and missed he was standing at the other end grinning. If I tried a really big heave and made no contact he would just lean on his bat and laugh out loud.
*Graham Dilley, who shared a stand of 117 from just 18 overs with ITB*

It seemed to me that the Australians had no real plan for bowling to Botham. Botham is always at his best when is given room for the stroke outside the off stump, never quite so certain when he is cramped for

room with the ball moving in at him from short of a
length and slightly outside off stump.
*Richie Benaud*

Botham isn't prepared to change for anyone or
anything, even the England captaincy. He played a
captain's innings one Test too late. He will fail often,
but equally he will dominate on occasions. Botham.
It's good to have you back!
*Rod Nicholson in Sydney's Daily Telegraph*

If we had won that match there was going to be no
more Botham, no more Gower, for the rest of the
series. Brearley's comeback would have meant
nothing.
*Kim Hughes*

We just always felt, every over, we're going to get him
out.
*Dennis Lillee*

It was hard to stand there in that crowd of cocky
Yorkshiremen and watch that.
*Dean Jones, tells Allan Border of his experience as a 20
year-old spectator at Headingley as ITB cut loose*

How do you think I felt out there in the middle then,
mate?
*AB's reply*

It was the lowest point I can remember in my cricket
career. It was a game we just couldn't lose.
*Allan Border*

Half a dozen of us went to Bryan's Fish and Chip restaurant up the road from the ground. We got a round of applause. Like a group of John the Baptists we were preparing a path for one greater than ourselves – for Ian and his family came in soon after.
*Mike Brearley on the night after ITB's 149 not out*

Even the Stock Exchange ceased trading, because everybody was watching the cricket on the TV.
*Bob Willis*

Third Test 1981: Day Five – Headingley. Post match interview.
*Mike Brearley:* 'Of course I let them force us to follow on. I knew Headingley would be a devilish pitch in the last day. It's like chess Richie, you've got to be two steps ahead of the opposition'.
Third Test, 1981: Day Four – Headingley. Ian Botham receives his pre-innings pep talk.
*Mike Brearley:* 'Five men out and we're still behind their first innings total. Basically we're buggered Ian. So, heads you poke around, tails you hit the bejesus out of it'.
*Fanzine 'George Davis is Innocent' alternative take on the miracle of '81*

'Are you listening to a radio, Easdale?'
'Yes sir'.
'Easdale, what do you think you are doing'.
'Sorry Sir'.
'Turn it up so the rest of us can hear'.
*Roderick Easdale remembers an unusual request from his*

*prep school teacher during ITB's 149*

Twelve years later I still remember Peter Willey getting out at fly slip, bringing Botham to the wicket. Then Dilley arriving ('92 runs behind with three wickets remaining', at the time meaningless and forgettable, now the most magical equation I've ever heard) and the ball rapidly departing to all four corners.
*Philip Cornwall*

There was a general feeling of disbelief afterwards. And a certain awe. We had seen an Australian win butchered from the strongest possible base. Yet we had also seen two of the finest performances in the modern era of Test match cricket.
*Alan McGilvray*

Life had been made hard for Botham in his latter Tests as leader. The very writers who had been boldly campaigning for him to be given the job not many months earlier were now cruelly consigning him to the rubbish patch.
*Bob Willis explains one of the reasons behind his anti-press outburst after the Headingley Test*

## EDGBASTON, THE FOURTH TEST
Sidestep queen.
*Mike Brearley's deliberate criticism of ITB's bowling action intended to get him fired up*

Somerset's giant bowled quicker than for some time, was straight and pitched the ball up, and one after

another five Australian batsmen walked into the point of the lance. The crowd, dotted with green and gold, were beside themselves with agony and ecstasy as, only twelve days after Headingley, history amazingly repeated itself.
*Wisden Cricketers' Almanack 1982 on ITB's 5-1 spell to win the game for England by 29 runs*

As I started my run up each time, the whole world was behind me.
*ITB*

BOTHAM 2 AUSTRALIA 1
*The Daily Express*

It was like being at a funeral. The depth of despair in the Australian quarters was every bit as morbid as that which moved Shirley Brooks to write the mock obituary notice which gave rise to the myth of the Ashes 99 years ago. In the Headingley press box even the heavy broadsheet merchants forgot their dignity and whooped like Red Indians at the fall of each Australian wicket. Silent wincing and muttered condolences for those whose accents were less rounded. The Australian batsmen were apparently stupefied by the atmosphere as the crowd roared Botham on and on.
*Sydney Daily Telegraph*

Botham seemed to have bewitched the Australians. They saw him coming and retreated into insecurity. As good a bowler as Botham is, the figures flattered

him enormously. He simply took advantage of a team broken in spirit, playing with a total lack of fight.
*Alan McGilvray*

The others are bowling better.
*ITB to Mike Brearley after his captain told him to begin his match-winning spell*

Keep it tight for Embers.
*Mike Brearley's instructions once he had persuaded ITB to bowl*

Why is it that Botham is always put on to bowl at the tailenders.
*Letter of complaint to Mike Brearley*

## OLD TRAFFORD, THE FIFTH TEST

Botham, who, with the pendulum starting to swing Australia's way in England's second innings, launched an attack on Lillee and Alderman which, for its ferocious yet effortless power and dazzling cleanness of stroke, can never surely have been bettered in a Test match, even by the legendary Jessop.
*Wisden Cricketers' Almanack on ITB's 118*

This was no slog, but two hours of sustained aggression which comprised shots of majesty and infinite power. In size it was breathtaking, in its mightiness it was almost frightening.
*David Lemmon*

They made more noise than if George Best had scored a hat trick down the road.

*ITB on the Old Trafford crowd*

What a marvellous way to go to a six.
*BBC TV commentator Jim Laker gets confused by the*
*mayhem as ITB strikes Ray Bright for six to bring up his*
*century*

Tav made it easier for me and played a marvellous
innings for the side. I don't think I could bat for seven
hours.
*ITB praises Chris Tavare who supported him in a stand of*
*149*

I will always remember that as being the most
exciting and emotional bit of cricket I have ever been
involved in.
*Chris Tavare (speaking after his retirement in 1993)*

I would cross mountains and swim rivers to be
present to see its like again.
*Sir Leonard Hutton on the Old Trafford innings*

Was Botham's innings the greatest ever?
*Front page headline in The Times*

Botham was able to scale heights beyond the reach of
ordinary men.
*John Woodcock*

I found it impossible to believe Botham could do
better than his innings at Headingley but yesterday
he managed it.
*Richie Benaud*

## REFLECTIONS ON BOTHAM'S ASHES

1981 – the Summer when Ian Botham made the impossible into the routine.
*Matthew Engel*

1981 was the defining season of Ian Botham's sporting life.
*John McCarthy*

It'll be remembered in 100 years – unfortunately.
*Kim Hughes on the 1981 Ashes series*

I think they'll talk about that Test series as long as cricket is played.
*Dickie Bird*

It was a great time to be playing, it was a great period in English history.
*ITB*

All names in the hat for captain in India by Friday please.
*ITB jokes about the number of Brearley's possible successors*

Surely, Botham is very much a contender for the captaincy. I can't believe his wonderful performances in the last three Tests have played him out of the running for the job.
*Richie Benaud*

I have never been sure of the theory that it is danger-ous to give your best player the captaincy, lest the

extra responsibility will cause him to lose his form (there are too many examples to the contrary) but Botham's case will certainly be quoted every time the question arises in future.
*Alan Gibson*

Without doubt, and whatever Botham's view may be, it was a relief to him to be captain no longer.
*Mike Brearley*

Brearley has paid me a nice compliment, comparing me to WG Grace. But he suggests I might not be that good if I'm allowed to take on the burden of the England captaincy again. I think he's wrong. It wasn't the captaincy that brought me down. I don't care what anybody says, no matter how good you are, you have a bad period in your career, and I genuinely believe that mine just happened to come at the time of my captaincy.
*ITB*

Take Botham out of our side and it would make us look very ordinary. We have an excellent relationship; he needs a father figure and I need a younger brother to help out.
*Mike Brearley*

It was the Brearley-Botham axis that produced the chemistry and the results – and Brearley thinks he knows one reason why; there was no competition between them. Brearley offered no challenge to Botham as an individual, which wasn't the case with

the intellectual Phil Edmonds. Botham was an outrageously gifted cricketer but wasn't known for long, thoughtful moments of introspection. Brearley's cricketing gifts were of a lower order. He is however, a deep thinker. Brearley could challenge Botham in a non threatening manner. In contrast to other Botham captains there was no antagonism or competition in the relationship.
*England Rugby captain Will Carling*

Could be I owe him more than he owes me.
*Mike Brearley*

# 1982-1985

## THE LIVING LEGEND

THE EVENTS OF THE 1981 ASHES SERIES HAD TRANSFORMED ITB from an admired and impressive Test cricketer into a sporting immortal – and he was still only 26. For the next four years, ITB was the biggest draw card in cricket, his batting often reaching unparalleled heights of brutal mastery. However, there were continuing signs that his unwillingness to control his weight was further undermining the effectiveness of his bowling. Just as disturbing were the first signs that the English tabloids, which had done so much to build up the Botham legend, were about to turn nasty.

## TEST RECORD: 1982-1985

| M | Inns | NO | Runs | HS | Av | 100s | 50s | Ct |
|---|---|---|---|---|---|---|---|---|
| 38 | 61 | 0 | 2432 | 208 | 39.87 | 5 | 15 | 33 |

| Ovs | Runs | W | Av | Best | 5w | 10w | SR |
|---|---|---|---|---|---|---|---|
| 1447 | 4762 | 141 | 33.77 | 8-103 | 8 | 0 | 61.57 |

## TO INDIA 1981-82

ITB departed for the away series against India as possibly the most famous cricketer in the world. The six match series has claims on being the most boring ever contested by an English team and ITB had little chance to shine. However, off the field one of the most shameful episodes of English cricket was beginning to take shape.

Botham had linked up with Gavaskar to promote tea, and nearly every Indian newspaper or magazine seemed to have the syndicated thoughts of Botham, Fletcher and many others. There was some talk in Bombay of the English players being a bit too greedy, but I could only admire their self-restraint. The game seemed to be used by almost every consumer company in town to sell its products.
*Mihir Bose*

As we assessed each batsman, Botham had one stock response – 'He can't play the short ball, I'll bounce him out'.
*Graham Gooch on ITB's contribution to team tactics*

Ian Botham stunned Central Zone yesterday with one of the fastest centuries of all time. He cracked 100 off just 48 balls in 50 minutes.
*The Sun*

Five of the tour party beside myself had already signed in principle to undertake a rebel tour. Botham

was especially keen.
*Geoff Boycott, one of the ring-leaders of the first 'rebel' tour to South Africa by English cricketers*

I was looking far more closely at the positions of Botham and Willis. At that stage they were both firm favourites to join the rebels and quickly it occurred to me that if a ban was handed down by Lord's, as it surely would be, England would suddenly be left without its two leading strike bowlers. For a young player like myself who had been in and out of the side for almost three years I could see the possibility of becoming a Test regular for years to come and it was an opportunity not to be missed whatever sort of money the South Africans were going to offer. Looking back, mine was a disastrous decision and one I was to regret for years. Botham pulled out during the Third Test in Bangalore, but his mind took some changing.
*Graham Dilley*

Ian Botham was offered £25,000 to play in the rebel tour of South Africa. He said no. Under the deal offered, Botham would have received a first instalment of £125,000 for joining the current four-week tour and a further £125,000 for a similar tour next year.
*The Sunday Times*

I could never look Viv Richards in the eye again.
*ITB's apparent reason for turning down the tour*

The suggestion that he [Botham] had opted out of the tour on moral grounds was unnecessary and puke-making. The players who went to South Africa know Botham's attitude full well and I doubt they will ever forget. 'I won't ever trust Both again', said Gooch and I reckon this feeling was unanimous.
*Geoff Boycott*

I was very moved when Ian Botham refused to go by stating that if he went he could never look me in the face again.
*Viv Richards in 1990*

That comment was attributed to me in a statement prepared on my behalf by Reg Hayter but which I never saw.
*ITB in 1993*

Reg Hayter and Alan Herd [ITB's solicitor] made it quite clear that if I went, financially I would be worse off and, more critically for me, I would certainly be barred from playing for England. I did not want to be seen supporting apartheid. Nevertheless, I would be a liar to say that finance didn't come into it.
*ITB in 1993*

## 1982

With the South African rebels banned for three years, England had a new-look side. However, its heart was still provided by ITB's all-round skills. 1982 turned out to be a classic year with ITB contesting the title of

'World's best all-rounder', first with India's Kapil Dev and then with Pakistan's Imran Khan. Off the field he was up to his usual tricks.

Ian Botham squeezed a smile between a sneezing attack of hay fever this week and coughed up an amazing revelation. 'No one will believe this, but I am actually allergic to grass'.
*The Sun*

Ian Botham has been asked to bat at No 5, a shrewd idea. This will encourage Ian to show his majestic range of shots rather then his prodigious hitting.
*Peter Roebuck*

The duel between Botham and Kapil was building up to quite a finish and Botham seemed to have settled it at The Oval when he made a massive 208. It was his highest Test score and a very quick double-century. 200 out of 220 balls in 268 minutes. One six off Doshi made a hole in the pavilion roof.
*Mihir Bose*

We have the makings of a very well-balanced side – the second best in the world, after the West Indians.
*ITB after England's 1-0 victory over India*

So on the last morning, England, with four wickets left, needed 29 to win, and Botham and Imran were thrown into direct confrontation. It would be quite unfair to suggest that either submerges team to

personal interest, but obviously there is rivalry in their opposition.
*John Arlott on the Third Test v Pakistan. ITB was out for 4, but England won by three wickets*

HE'D RATHER BE OUT DRIVING HIS SAAB
In even the greatest sporting careers, there are days when things don't go entirely according to plan. On such occasions, it would hardly be surprising if Ian Botham's thoughts turned to his Saab Turbo. Behind the wheel he doesn't have to worry about spin: Saabs are legendary for their road-holding. Pace is never a problem either: a Turbo is good deal quicker than Michael Holding. So when he is bowling along the fast lane of the motorway, it's extremely unlikely that he'll be caught.
*Copy for an advert for Saab cars (one of ITB's sponsors) depicting ITB having his off stump knocked back*

I hope to do some rally driving. I'm not going to allow other people to run my life.
*ITB after crashing two of his sponsored Saabs on the same day*

We do not like him rushing around at breakneck speeds like this. We shall be having a quiet word with Ian.
*Somerset chairman Roy Kerslake*

I attended a boating party in Bath with the Somerset and Indian cricketers. It had been a quiet trip and as

we returned under the Pulteney Bridge, Ian set aside his beer can and, rising, seized Nigel Popplewell and unceremoniously tossed his Somerset team-mate out of the boat and into the river. We were mostly shocked, but the cricketers must have expected Botham to leave such a mark on the boat trip. Popplewell had taken his shoes off.
*ITB biographer Dudley Doust*

## TO AUSTRALIA 1982-1983

After the heroics of 1981, ITB's arrival in Australia was awaited with almost messianic fervour. However, ITB had been piling on the weight again and, as in the summer of 1980, his bowling suffered.

I notice that some commentators are beginning to sharpen their pencils to record the decline of Ian Botham – but surely not the experienced ones? You are either naive or foolish if you think that Ian will leave Australia without making a considerable impact on the series.
*England team-mate Vic Marks*

It dawned on him that he has to practice getting a bit more nip into his bowling.
*Captain Bob Willis on ITB before the second Test*

You know a few Afrikaans swear words. Have a go at him.
*ITB to Alan Lamb as fellow South African Kepler Wessels hits 162 on his debut for Australia*

A waste of ten good pokes, but it was worth it.
*ITB's verdict on a practical joke which involved inserting ten condoms into the fingers of Derek Randall's batting gloves*

We had to let Australia get within four runs. That was the only time Botham would perform. I couldn't put him on any earlier.
*Bob Willis after England had won the Fourth Test by three runs*

We reduced him from the man we knew in other tests, who could walk on water, to a normal human being.
*Australian captain Greg Chappell on the 1982-1983 Ashes series*

What worries me is that we could have seen the end of Ian as a high quality opening bowler.
*Freddie Trueman*

The umpiring on this tour has not been very good. In fact, it was so bad at times you felt we had to get 14 of their wickets and they only had to get ten of ours.
*ITB*

I feel Botham went into the series under-prepared because of a somewhat casual approach to the early matches. The sight of Botham's extremely ineffectual use of the new ball must have been demoralising to a side with only one proven penetrative fast bowler.
*Daily Telegraph cricket correspondent Michael Carey*

The biggest letdown of all was Ian Botham. It comes hard to have to say it, but it should come as no surprise to him. He didn't make the runs I had hoped of him and his bowling was seldom dangerous. If he is to contribute again significantly at Test level, he may have to change his approach or elect to concentrate on only one part of his game – probably batting.
*Bob Willis*

He certainly suffered some pain in his back towards the end of last season. He has done the best to overcome that and it's difficult because he's a naturally heavy man. But if the problem continues, he should think of concentrating on his batting at the expense of his bowling.
*Viv Richards*

## 1983

As England contested the Third World Cup and tackled New Zealand in a four match Test series, the questions marks over ITB's previously unquestioned role in the England (and Somerset) team began to multiply.

If I were Ian I would put regaining the Test captaincy aside. I know he thinks he has something to prove, and being Botham, that nags his thoughts. But if I were in his place, I would let the ambition drift away and concentrate on thoroughly enjoying myself. Botham should be left alone to play his natural game. I would dearly love to see him in a powerful England side, with the threat of failure less important.
*Sir Leonard Hutton*

Botham is not half the bowler he was two or three
years ago.
*Christopher Martin-Jenkins*

Which three players would you replace him with?
*England captain Bob Willis' answer to the press when it
was suggested that ITB should be dropped after New
Zealand beat England at Headingley*

Somerset officials had realised that Botham was
bound to be made captain in 1984, realised what a
potentially unwise move this would be and yet were
not resolute enough to avoid it.
*Peter Roebuck*

I'm not going to mention names, but players are
having to cheat to make the ball swing. Players are
picking the seam because the balls we use these days
don't swing as much as they used to.
*ITB, nine years before the ball-tampering controversy*

People try to tell us there is no difference. They must
think we came in on the last banana boat. These balls
are different. But they won't have it at Lord's. All the
lads I have talked to said that these balls are a waste
of time. Certainly that is one reason why my bowling
faltered last year.
*ITB on the balls used on the county circuit*

Spurning the possibility of turning his score of 96 into
a century, Botham deliberately played for a tie, which

was sufficient for victory over Middlesex, the season's most successful county.
*The Daily Telegraph on ITB's match-winning contribution in the NatWest semi-final*

Hundreds do not worry me. I worry about wins for Somerset and England.
*ITB after the match*

Ian Botham is ready to defy Lord's and play a Fourth Division soccer game two days before he flies off on tour with England.
*The Sun reports on ITB's desire to turn out for Scunthorpe before flying off on tour to New Zealand and Pakistan*

Don't be so daft – for England's sake and your team-mates. To risk injury like this on the eve of a major tour is silly. I want you on that plane next Thursday in prime nick – and I'll be very upset if you're not.
*England tour manager Alan Smith reacts to ITB's decision*

Ian wants me to pick him and I feel he has the right to play.
*Scunthorpe manager Allan Clarke*

Nothing would give me greater satisfaction than to get into the Scunthorpe side and help them win promotion into the Third Division. That really would be a dream come true.
*ITB*

## TO NEW ZEALAND AND PAKISTAN 1983-84

The sex and drugs allegations which beset this tour are detailed in the Tabloid Hell chapter. During the Tests that ITB played before being invalided home his genius shone only intermittently.

Willis was often accused of letting Botham bowl too much, particularly at Richard Hadlee when his 99 proved so decisive on a bad wicket during the Christchurch Test. But I believe Willis had such faith in Botham that he was happy to leave him at one end for long periods so that he would only have to concentrate as captain on getting things right at the other end.
*Graham Dilley*

It seemed only too absurdly appropriate that the team should spend its one off day between the Second and Third Tests [against Pakistan] signing affidavits for Botham's hastily dispatched solicitor, to the effect that he had returned home for reasons of heath, not of discipline.
*Nick Cook and Neville Scott*

It's been a jinxed tour. We have lost our first-ever Test series in New Zealand. We lost the first Test against Pakistan and the first-one day international in Lahore. We have been hit by these [sex and drugs] allegations and I am on my way home with a busted knee. And you ask me how I feel.
*ITB to a Daily Mail journalist as he returns home*

## 1984

The summer's five match series against the West Indies was a disaster for England who lost every game. They were even made to look pretty ordinary by Sri Lanka, playing their first Test in the UK. ITB's season, apart from his 8-103 at Lord's, was unnaturally quiet.

There is no reason why Botham should not be bowling well and taking Test wickets at Test level when he is 36 years of age in 1991. After all, Keith Miller gave one of his greatest bowling exhibitions in the Lord's Test of 1956 at the same age. In Botham's case, I think he needs first of all to have treatment for his back and then to find a way to utilise a bowling action which gives him his best chance of taking wickets and, at the same time, protecting his back.
*Richie Benaud*

What the hell's going on now? What's he bowling. Something's got to be done, this can't go on.
*Chairman of selectors Peter May, rather distressed at ITB's decision to bowl off-spin as the Test against Sri Lanka wound down into a draw*

Anybody who dyes his hair that colour deserves to be caught on the boundary.
*Taunton spectator on ITB's blonde rinse*

## 1985

Refreshed and recharged after a winter off, ITB looked forward to the arrival of Allan Border's Australian's.

Only a further drugs scandal darkened his mood.

I do hope Ian Botham does not play for England
again. I have a young family – enough said?
*M A Grantham's letter to Wisden Cricket Monthly after
ITB's conviction for possessing cannabis*

How I sympathise with Mr Grantham in his paternal
desire to protects his offspring from Ian Botham. My
own experience only serves to illustrate the harmful
effects of succumbing to the dreadful weed. In May
1968 I smoked my first and last 'joint' and I am certain
that therein lies the source of my subsequent misfortune. Although I have continually held myself in
readiness to open the innings for my country, the call
has never come. Thus in surrendering to one moment
of sensual pleasure, I robbed my fellow Englishmen of
the chance to witness the rebirth of English cricket, an
event that was delayed until July 20, 1981. Let me
assure Mr Grantham that not only does the occasional
joint totally expunge any natural cricket ability one
may possess, but it also has another side effect, which
will soon become apparent to the medical profession,
viz, a feeling of sudden and uncontrollable hostility
towards pompous sods.
*Another WCM reader, M R Frost, replies*

I urge Botham to follow the example of Steve Davis
and concentrate all his energy on what he does best,
while keeping the off-the-field distractions to a mini-
mum.
*E J Brack*

A positive bonus.
*Christopher Martin Jenkins' verdict on ITB's absence from an England side that beat India in a memorable series during the winter of 1984-85*

I think we have a team now because Ian Botham is no longer playing for England. It does appear to me that he has probably been a disrupting influence upon the team.
*Denis Compton*

I don't feel angry about Denis Compton's comments. Just pity that a great ex-Test cricketer like that should feel the need to have a go at present-day profession-als. That sickened me. It's a terrible shame to see someone like that existing by pulling other people apart. I only know that when I retire I won't go around taking cheap shots at the players of the day. I've never done anything to Denis Compton. He's never played or toured with me so I don't know exactly what he's basing his criticisms on.
*ITB replies*

Botham's innings ended with him trying a reverse sweep against Matthews but missing and being bowled. It was not the smartest stroke to play to an off-spinner on a turning pitch, and one specifically designed to bring out the bile in those cricket sages who prefer to observe the cracks in the Botham canvas rather than the masterful brushstrokes.
*Matthew Engel on the first One-day International*

I have thumbed through the MCC coaching manual
and found that no such stroke exists.
*Chairman of selectors Peter May criticises ITB's reverse
sweep*

One of my tamer dismissals. I've got myself out in far
more macabre ways over the years.
*ITB's reaction to the same shot*

Ah, Botham! He has been scoring a run a ball or better
all season. The Jessop of the age. But that is strictly an
average. He appears to have given up the routine
business of running ones and twos except as an
occasional concession to his partners. He came out
yesterday 40 minutes after lunch. For the next hour
Botham used his bat like a machine gun. His 60 took
51 balls; but 52 of the runs came off only 12 of them.
When Border brought himself on, like an Anzac
subaltern hurling himself uselessly at the Turkish
lines, the temptation to reverse sweep must have been
irresistible. Botham resisted, went for a conventional
sweep and a huge straight six. You can stuff your
nostalgia; Botham was brilliant.
*Matthew Engel on the First Test*

Botham would even watch the first day at The Oval
from the matey comfort of the Australian dressing
room. Another example of declining standards, what?
*Rob Steen*

This series was the quickest he has ever bowled for

England. His efforts with the bat and ball and in the field were outstanding, and I think he made the real difference between the two teams.
*David Gower after England clinched the Ashes at the Oval*

Ashes to Ashes, dust to dust; if Botham doesn't get you, Ellison must.
*Banner at The Oval*

For Botham the winter of 1985 was to be a watershed. By now his dreams had moved from heroism to fantasy.
*Peter Roebuck*

Botham remained an enigma during the summer. He had a new agent, there was exaggerated talk of a showbusiness career and some sartorial eccentricity from him, allied to marketing considerations. Some of the his mates couldn't quite fathom which direction, professionally, he was going.
*David Foot*

Mr Botham has decided that it is time he grew up. He has the choice – he can be Freddie Trueman, or he can be an international figure like Arnold Palmer.
*ITB's new agent Tim Hudson*

Attack with Botham Trousers.
*Advertisement for new range of ITB-sponsored sportswear*

It always amazes me that the French and Italians are

regarded as the trend-setters in fashion when in fact the designs that come from this country are as original as anywhere and often in front of the Americans. The beauty of this country is that, to a large extent, you can still do what you want and dress how you like.
*ITB fashion expert*

We realise he's not going to be Lord Olivier, but perhaps King of the B Movies.
*Tim Hudson on his attempts to make ITB a film star*

My own doubts are not that he cannot cope with the auto-cue, but that asthma and related sinus problems may cause diction problems.
*Derek Wyatt on ITB the actor*

Why should I slog my guts on the cricket pitch when I can make my fortune doing other things.
*ITB*

I've done the six.
*ITB's tongue-in-cheek reply to an HTV interviewer's question: 'Would you rather hit a six off the Australians or attend an opening night of your own film in Hollywood?'*

I've done the first six times and I never made any money out of it.
*ITB's remarks as reported by the BBC*

Superstar cricketer Ian Botham has landed a million-dollar part in a film. He will appear alongside Oliver

Reed as murderer and rapist. The Australian-produced thriller will be shot in New Zealand. Botham's agent Tim Hudson said last night: 'We've just received the contract and we're ready to sign. Ian will be guaranteed 1 million US dollars and he can't wait to get cracking.'
*The Sun*

'Rambotham' fever hit Australia last night. *The Sun* sparked an amazing reaction after exclusively breaking the news that Ian Botham was set to star in a Rambo-style role alongside Oliver Reed. The film's producer, Gary Rhodes, made a frantic call to *The Sun* offices from his home in Brisbane. He told me: 'I woke up this morning with half a dozen camera crews and scores of newsmen and photographers camped on my front doorstep. It seems that everybody in Australia wants to know where they can see Ian Botham on the big screen. Ian may be a hero to all the Poms, but here he's public enemy No.1.'
*The Sun*

At the end of the 1985 season, ITB embarked on a walk from John O'Groats to Land's End to raise money for children suffering from Leukemia.

If anybody would like to question my motives (for the Charity Walk) face to face, I'd happily bend his nose for him.
*ITB on suggestions that he was a self-publicist*

I don't know who you are, but there's ever such a lot of people following you.
*Elderly woman to ITB on the Charity Walk*

Occupants of this age-old literary establishment take their eyes off the play only at their peril. We have all seen Ian Botham throw out a challenging look in our direction and then aim at our typewriters.
*David Foot describes the dangers of residing in the Taunton press box when ITB was playing*

# 1986-1993

## THE LONG GOODBYE

The Somerset Affair

The Australian (Mis)Adventure

The Alpine Walk

DESPITE THE FACT THAT ITB CONTINUED TO PLAY FIRST-CLASS cricket for another eight years, and Test cricket for another seven, his effectiveness as a World Class all-rounder came to an end in 1985 when he was just 30 years old. In stark contrast to his rise, which had been spectacular and breath-taking in its speed, his decline was tortuous and drawn out. But ever so often, there were flashes of the old Botham.

## BATTING RECORD IN TESTS 1977-1985

| M | Inns | NO | Runs | HS | Av | 100s | 50s |
|---|---|---|---|---|---|---|---|
| 79 | 125 | 3 | 4409 | 208 | 36.14 | 13 | 20 |

## BATTING RECORD IN TESTS 1986-1992

| M | Inns | NO | Runs | HS | Av | 100s | 50s |
|---|---|---|---|---|---|---|---|
| 23 | 36 | 3 | 791 | 138 | 23.97 | 1 | 2 |

## BOWLING RECORD IN TESTS 1977-1985

| Ovs | Runs | W | Av | Best | 5w | 10w | SR |
|---|---|---|---|---|---|---|---|
| 3065.2 | 9046 | 343 | 26.37 | 8-34 | 25 | 4 | 53.62 |

## BOWLING RECORD IN TESTS 1986-1992

| Ovs | Runs | W | Av | Best | 5w | 10w | SR |
|---|---|---|---|---|---|---|---|
| 570.4 | 1832 | 40 | 45.80 | 5-41 | 2 | 0 | 85.60 |

Firmly back in his position as the nation's best known and best loved cricketer after his Ashes exploits and his John O'Groats – Land's End walk, ITB travelled with the England tour party to take on the mighty West Indies in the Caribbean. England and ITB's hopes were high, but only cruel disappointment and disillusionment lay ahead.

He will quit three-day cricket after this coming season. From then on it will be one-day cricket and Test matches.
*The about-to-be-sacked Tim Hudson*

Where the Botham business went wrong was with him trying to bowl as a strike bowler as he had done against Australia the previous summer. He was neither in the right sort of form, nor, in all honesty, was he fit enough.
*David Gower*

The Press-box had already placed me on the gallows so I was just telling you people you might as well go the whole way now and pull the rope.
*ITB explains his gesture as he left the field after being dismissed after seven balls in the Second Test*

Nobody even talks about the game. We're three Tests down, we're being stuffed out of sight and some of them don't seem to care about it. I was very disappointed by Botham's attitude.
*Pat Pocock*

Botham tried to fight fire with fire and flashed away
for 21 runs when he might have taken a more cautious
approach on a wicket where one could not have
known how high the next ball would bounce.
*Joel Garner on ITB's innings in the Third Test which*
*England lost by an innings and 30 runs*

Botham's kamikaze approach would have been
extraordinary in any other batsman. His aim in this
hopeless crisis seemed to be to smash a rapid 149 not
out and let Thomas or somebody – his desperate self?
– follow up with 8 for 43.
*David Frith on the same innings*

Check my Test career and I defy anyone to find an
instance in which I was out first ball trying to whack a
West Indian quickie for six in a crisis.
*ITB (in 1995)*

Oh God, now they're stabbing Botham in the front.
*Matthew Engel after the tabloids break the broken bed story*

It was commonly believed among the team that the
bed Ian had so infamously been accused of breaking
in a bout of passion was actually damaged by Les
Taylor sitting on it.
*David Smith*

Botham complained to David Gower that colleagues
were blaming him for the over-zealousness of the
press, which was actually quite near the mark; the

pettiness could hardly have reached such heights had he not been there.
*Rob Steen*

I said I was fed up with us being so matey with the West Indies while we were playing and that we should remember they were the enemy on the pitch. Now Both took this very personally, mainly because of his close friendship with Viv, and got a bit uptight. Then Phil Edmonds chipped in, saying he agreed with me and before we knew it everything went off. I hadn't meant to start an international incident, but I suppose I did have Both in mind and it needed to be said. He always had his arm round Viv during matches but I'm sure deep down Viv was laughing at that because the West Indies were intent on doing us.
*David Smith*

ITB returned from the Caribbean, to a series of fresh controversies and yet another comeback.

Let's not be mealymouthed about it: his discomfort and slide from grace have given immense pleasure to many who envy his talents, resent his commercial power and are jealous of his sometimes blind courage. Without being blasphemous, it might even be claimed that he is being crucified for the sins of many. If that be so, let the broom sweep like a tornado through the game. Let all who smoke pot, drink more than a pint, cheat on their wives, drive dangerously or deceive the Inland Revenue also be expelled from the game.

*David Frith on ITB's two month ban for admitting to smoking pot*

If the TCCB did not know until yesterday that he smoked marijuana, it was in the minority among those closely connected with the game.
*John Woodcock*

Gin-soaked old dodderers.
*ITB on the English cricket selectors*

My blood boiled when I saw Walker sitting on the settee next to Ian Botham, chatting about all he was going to do for him. Walker wrecked my life.
*British Judo star Brain Jacks on Bev Walker, ITB's new manager*

I think Bev's the best in the business. He's the best thing Botham could have.
*Gymnast and TV celebrity Susan Dando*

Ian Botham, just back from his suspension for drug use, came and hit 175 not out in 27 overs of a Sunday game with 13 sixes. He was watched by one of the County's biggest crowds in years.
*Matthew Engel in his history of Northamptonshire*

For pointless hours in Antigua, Botham bowled and bowled in an attempt to get that wicket. Now one suspension, four months and a million column inches later he had done it at the first attempt. Don't ask for

a cricketing explanation: there is none. We are into the paranormal.
*Matthew Engel reports on Botham becoming the highest wicket-taker in Test cricket*

The lone spectator in the Members' Enclosure who booed him when he came on to bowl at 12.12 pm was abruptly ordered by his neighbours to 'shut up'. Botham's first ball, guided to Graham Gooch by Bruce Edgar, left him with no option but to comply. And Gooch's first words to Botham were: 'Who writes your script?'
*The Sunday Times*

It had taken just one ball from the 30-year old all-rounder to seek and gain immediately the nation's forgiveness for his past sins.
*Peter Smith*

Lillee will always be a better bowler than me.
*ITB after breaking Lillee's record*

## THE SOMERSET AFFAIR

Outraged by Somerset's decision to dispense with the services of Viv Richards and Joel Garner, ITB decided to leave the county.

Botham believed he could swing the ordinary people behind him, as he had done on his celebrated sponsored walk. In fact members realised he was not the issue and his stance was scarcely mentioned.

*Somerset captain Peter Roebuck on ITB's threats to leave the county if Richards and Garner were sacked*

Someone put around the notion that I was a bad influence on Ian Botham. How ridiculous. Ian, more than anyone else I have ever met, is his own man.
*Viv Richards*

Some people see a tricoloured sweat-band on a fellow's wrists and all of a sudden he's a lunatic radical Rasta with a licence to kill. They succeeded in building up this image of Viv Richards' influence on Botham: so that when Both had his problems with the media during the West Indies tour, it would seem like Viv Richards and the West Indians were making a mess of the blue-eyed blond. But Botham is his own man. Somewhere behind the committee's decision lies the feeling that if they got rid of Richards and Garner the Botham problem would go away. Well it did; but not in the way that they thought it would.
*Joel Garner*

Botham did not feel at home in the club, did not feel loved, did not feel wanted. At Somerset, because he was away so often, he could find little companionship.
*Peter Roebuck*

Botham informed Richards that he would be leaving the county at the end of the 1986 season. After Roebuck's intervention the threat seemed to recede for

a while, but after returning from his drugs-linked playing ban and being told that he would have to play a second XI match to prove his fitness, he once again said he would leave and this time take Richards with him. Such threats can only have given ammunition to those among the club's administration who were plotting to replace Richards and Garner. 'Was it not obvious', they may have argued, 'that Viv and Joel show greater loyalty to Botham than they do to Somerset?' And given the fierce loyalty shown by Botham towards the overseas players when they were sacked, it would not be surprising if the two West Indians privately argued that the great England all-rounder deserved their loyalty more than the club which was eventually to dismiss them in such a cursory manner.
*Alastair McLellan*

Judas
*The sign hung on Peter Roebuck's locker by ITB*

## TO AUSTRALIA 1986-1987

Despite the heroics of the Oval Test, ITB's position in the Test side was still hotly debated by every pub know-all and newspaper pundit. The Somerset affair had only  intensified the carnival of controversy which continued to surround him. But the Australian's were ITB's favourite opponents and he had not finished with them yet.

On the way to the Gabba this morning my taxi driver said that Botham was bound to score a century. He'd

seen him in the lobby and remarked upon his aura of
confidence.  He was right. His back foot shots were as
perfect as Hammond's. He was more erratic off the
front foot than is recommended in the books, but he is
also a wicket-taker and can afford these little extrava-
gances. This was an innings directed as much at the
Somerset captain, as at his Australian opponents.
*Peter Roebuck (the Somerset captain) describes ITB's 137 at
Brisbane during the First Test*

The hefty amounts of cash raised was all put towards
the presents which the social committee had decided
each player should receive at the Christmas lunch.
Some of the best examples are team secrets – Botham
received a packet of grass seed.
*Graham Dilley*

Bollinger, the champagne company, were prepared to
pay 10,000 Australian dollars just for Ian to appear as
a celebrity in their Marquee at the Melbourne Cup.
*The Sun*

It's a bit like Steve Davis having his favourite snooker
cue stolen or someone removing Elton John's piano
just before the concert starts.
*ITB after that bat with which he had scored over 1500 Test
runs was stolen*

You're welcome to use one of my bats  They're the
same make, but might not be quite as heavy as you
like.
*Aussie captain Allan Border offers his help*

My mother could have hit it harder with a fucking shovel.
*Elton John after ITB was dismissed for a duck in the Fifth Test*

I couldn't carry him, so it was push, pull and drag. I didn't get the full use of my right arm back for two days.
*John Emburey describes how he 'assisted' a drunken ITB up the back stairs of a Perth hotel at 5am. ITB scored 70 against West Australia the following day*

Botham has taken DeFreitas under his wing and is showing him the way. DeFreitas has brought life to the most bloody minded of the cricket professionals and it is healthy for Botham to guide him. It is better for him to have a protege than lots of bosom pals. And as long as DeFreitas has the sense to plough his own furrow he can benefit from this friendship. Botham is giving to him things he has not given to young cricketers for years.
*Peter Roebuck*

A great deal was made of the fact that Ian Botham took Daffy (DeFreitas) under his protective wing and that Daffy received an invaluable early lesson from one of world's three best all-rounders. Now while this, up to a point, is perfectly true, there was also an adverse effect that Both can have in these sort of circumstances. Ian's methods have always been slightly unorthodox and his anti-authoritarian views

on life in general would probably have been absorbed by Daffy.
*David Gower*

DeFreitas says that Botham has been nothing but a positive influence on him, getting him to approach the game more professionally. During one 1987 Leicestershire v Somerset game Botham noticed that DeFreitas was falling away in his delivery. During the over he shouted to him, 'Come on Daffy, get your shoulder upright and put your back into it.' That night, over a few beers, Botham began a masterclass of seam bowling, giving DeFreitas a strongly worded lecture.
*Patrick Murphy*

The editorial typified the current media obsession with this dramatic, mercurial cricketer, at the expense of a balanced view. This is neither good for his ego nor fair to others.
*EW Swanton on a report in the Independent which he believed gave undue prominence to ITB's efforts in a World Series Cup game*

There's not much you can do about Botham in that mood. It might have been a decent game without him.
*Allan Border after ITB's dominating performance in the first final of the World Series Cup*

I get quite excited when people write me off.
*ITB reflecting on his heroic performance in the WSC final*

The clue to this series, as to many others, lay in the relationship between Botham and his captain. Gatting demanded that Botham work hard in the nets.  From the start of the tour he treated him like any other player, and this time Botham's genius was incorporated into the team's effort, rather than living independently of it. Gatting deserves the congratulations of every English cricketer for having handled Botham better than any other previous tour captain.
*Peter Roebuck*

Ian Botham has sacked his manager Bev Walker. I understand that Botham has been upset by Walker's comments linking him with Minor County Northumberland just before he signed for Worcester.
*Chris Lander, Daily Mirror*

They are offering the sort of money no first-class county could afford.
*Bev Walker on Northumberland's offer*

Tom Byron (Botham's Australian manager) has clinched a number of lucrative sponsorship deals, including;  a £40,000 deal with a top food chain, a £40,000 property firm contract,  a £30,000 tie-up with the Ansett airline, a £30,000 deal with a major brewery, a £20,000 link with the Saab car company and a £20,000 deal for a top wine firm.
*The Sun*

## 1987

Two surprising additions to the Worcestershire staff

came shortly before the start of the 1987 season: Graham Dilley and Ian Botham. The moves were not universally approved, but they were to have a profound effect upon the future of Worcestershire cricket. Importantly for Worcestershire both men had tasted success whereas no-one else in the side had the experience of winning a competition. They brought to Worcestershire a new dimension and Botham, in particular, brought the quality of self-belief.
*David Lemmon*

## 1987-1988: THE AUSTRALIAN (MIS)ADVENTURE

While England toured Pakistan and New Zealand, ITB headed down under to play for Queensland. Big, big mistake.

Botham plans to spend a lot of his time in the near future playing in Australia and I'm sure that it will be good for him. It can be a sort of fresh start – new situation, new friends, new media. I hope he does not allow himself to be dragged into the media syndrome and recreate in Australia what he would rather leave behind in Britain.
*Geoff Boycott*

Botham and Queensland were made for each other – big, brassy, noisy and aggressively masculine.
*Peter Roebuck*

It's a disgrace Botham hasn't been called up by England – the selectors will regret it. England really

need him with their current lot of Joe Bloggs's.
*Jeff Thomson on England's decision not to select ITB for the one-off Bicentennial Test in Australia*

Queensland were the team to watch for the early part of the season and it was Ian Botham they flocked to see, with home attendances nearly triple those of 1986-87.
*Chris Harte*

He has inspired everyone and his appearance has pulled in the biggest crowds seen at Shield matches for years. He has my backing and the support of the whole Queensland squad who hope off-the-field incidents are not going to stop him coming back.
*Queensland captain Allan Border after ITB was charged with assault following an alleged brawl on a Brisbane to Perth flight*

If that man had kept his nose out of an argument that had nothing to do with him, between Allan Border and myself, none of this would have happened.
*ITB's justification for seizing his fellow passenger in an (alleged) headlock*

It seems rather strange to me that a court of law fines you $A800 yet the cricket authorities seem to feel they can fine you a lot more. Five thousand dollars is about 50 quid [actually, it is about £2000] at the current rate of sterling, so I'm not really too bothered.
*ITB on the fine levied by the Queensland Cricket Association*

Bully boy Ian Botham was told last night, 'We don't need you in Queensland'. Australia's former Test hero Peter Burge said 'I will be glad when he's gone. I'm bitterly disappointed by the way he has behaved. I wish we'd never got him here'.
*The Sun*

If I had done something terrible and brought their game into major disrepute they would never ask me to play there again. I believe they are looking forward to me coming back. If nothing else it brightens up a dull day.
*ITB*

You know Both. It is often this sort of thing that revs him up.
*Worcestershire chairman Duncan Fearnley on ITB's airline bust-up*

I think questions must be asked before Ian represents England again. The way he's going he will destroy himself with a succession of unsportsmanlike acts.
*Tom Graveney*

I like the bugger. He's a grand lad. It's just a pity he spoils himself. But this might bring him to his senses.
*Brian Close on ITB's sacking by Queensland*

The Australian public have backed him to the hilt, so have his sponsors.
*ITB's Australian manager Tom Byron*

We feel a little let down over what has happened. We had planned a heavy advertising campaign with Ian, but that had to be shelved when all the trouble blew up. He got through three-quarters of this tour and then he went mad. I just can't understand it. We have to keep him in check, but that is not always easy.
*Ted Marwick, managing director of Botham's sponsor Carphone*

A fortnight that Ian Botham doubtless will be keen to forget began on March 14 when the news broke that his Great Dane, Kirri, which had escaped from Botham's Yorkshire home, had been shot dead by a farmer after savaging a flock of sheep, killing six.
*Wisden Cricket Monthly*

Mr Botham has not complied with certain provisions of the contract between himself and the association. Consequently, it has been decided that Mr Botham be advised that the agreement is terminated.
*Statement issued by the Queensland Cricket Association*

I have every intention of going back (to Australian state cricket).
*ITB after hearing of Queensland's decision*

Ian loves Australia and the Aussies love him more than ever after the way he has been treated by Queensland. That's why he will be going back.
*Tom Byron*

Why don't you all go and fuck yourselves, you're

trying to destroy me. You bastards have been out to get me since I arrived. All you Aussies are a bunch of hicks who don't know the first thing about cricket. No one should be subjected to this kind of hounding. Leave me alone. As far as I'm concerned you can all drop dead. I'm sick to death of this kind of treatment and won't be coming back here again. You can all go to hell.

*ITB rails at journalists as he catches plane out of Australia*

I backed Ian as much as I could, but he didn't help himself by his lack of remorse. He should have apologised, said he had been stupid. If he had done that, I'm sure he would have been invited back by Queensland.

*Allan Border*

He let cricket down. He let Queensland cricket down. He let Australian cricket down. I think the QCA made the right decision.

*Australian Prime Minister Bob Hawke*

I find it hard to understand the holier than holy people. They are ex-players who five years after they finish the game start preaching, 'you shouldn't do this and you shouldn't do that'. Well, they seem to forget I played 'em. I know how they used to play up and fall over in bars.

*ITB*

## 1988: THE ALPINE WALK

Botham being Botham, his idea of relaxing after the tempestuous season with Queensland was to walk across the Alps with a couple of elephants. His second charity walk was noticeably less successful than his first, largely because the French and Italians didn't know who he was, and ITB was plagued throughout the whole footsore journey by persistent tabloid press efforts to whip up a scandal.

My priorities are in this order; one, the happiness and welfare of my family, two, the 700km between here and Turin, three, the money my walk will hopefully raise for the Leukemia Research Fund. Finally, and perhaps most importantly [sic], the successful fulfilment of my remaining two years of my contract with Worcestershire. I intend to honour my responsibilities in every regard so that I will be free to voice revelations that will make your hair stand on end.
*ITB at pre-walk press conference*

Ian Botham has been voted the 'Pipesmoker of the Year' for 1988, and will be represented with the trophy – a specially-made pipe – by last year's winner, Barry Norman, at a luncheon at Lord's on April 27. Meanwhile, Botham's trans-Alpine walk has run into a few problems. Arrangements for transporting the three accompanying elephants over the river Rhone are proving difficult, while French animal-rights activists, led by Brigette Bardot, are said to be planning a demonstration alongside the walk, protest-

ing about 'cruelty to elephants'.
*Wisden Cricket Monthly 1988*

Brigette Bardot is reportedly exercised by the
Elephants' coming ordeal. To which Botham has
retorted: 'I care about kids, not kittens'.
*The Guardian*

What is wrong with that kind of an arsehole? At the
end of the day, I hope that neither that bastard nor his
family get leukemia.
*ITB on a journalist he believed had written an
inaccurate story about the walk*

Whatever I do, wherever I go, there is always some
fucking joker trying to bring me down. For God's
sake, this walk is going to raise millions for people
who are dying. There is not the slightest possibility of
the elephants suffering, so go and tell Bill Travers –
whoever he is – to get stuffed.
*ITB comments on the arrival on the walk of Bill Travers,
director of animal welfare group Zoo Check*

The English Platini.
*French newspaper's description of ITB*

Whereas Hannibal, 2,000 years ago, came to this
country to bring war, you have come to bring with
you messages of hope.
*Piazza Castello, mayoress of Turin*

Back in England, ITB rejoined Worcestershire, but his

season was soon ended by a serious back injury.

Probably the fittest cricketer in England.
*Worcestershire team doctor Steve Carroll after ITB's return*

Worcestershire's lead was consolidated when maximum points were taken in the game against Hampshire at New Road. Hick and Curtis scored centuries of contrasting style, and Botham's helicopter, taking the great man for convalescence, dipped in salute over the ground on the first afternoon.
*David Lemmon*

## 1989

By now ITB, his bowling reduced to little more than medium pace, was a bit part player in the England Test side. He played three Tests against the visiting Australian's, but scored just 62 runs and captured only three wickets.

There were all the usual references in the build-up to the Test to Both's 149 not out at Headingley in 1981 and it gets up your nose a bit really. After all that was only one brilliant knock and England's been living off it for a long, long time.
*Allan Border before the Third Test at Headingley*

Before we even began the discussions, I was instruct-ed to discount both of them. I think both Ted Dexter and Micky Stewart wanted to get away from the champagne-set image which had been around for a

few years.
*Graham Gooch explains why Gower and Botham were not selected for the West Indies tour*

In my heart I wish the boys well, but my brain tells me five-nil.
*ITB's forecast for the 1989/90 West Indies tour. ITB was not selected and England lost a hard fought series (2-1)*

The master blaster has become a past master. Botham the blockbuster has declined in public popularity to B-movie status.
*EJ Brack*

## 1990

With ITB firmly on the International cricketing sidelines, he looked for other ways to earn a crust.

Bloody awful stuff – it doesn't get you drunk and you feel like Mike Gatting.
*The ever-diplomatic ITB makes a passing reference to the sponsors of his first roadshow, Dansk low alcohol larger*

He claimed Gatting's tour was responsible for the release of Nelson Mandela.
*Cricket fanzine The Name of the Rose reports on the ITB roadshow*

Is it true you are hung like a rhino?
*Question to ITB during one of his roadshows*

We roomed together for six wonderful years until the

wives put a stop to it.
*ITB, during his roadshow, on Allan Lamb*

## TO NEW ZEALAND AND AUSTRALIA 1992

It seemed that ITB had disappeared for ever from the international scene until he made what was to be his final comeback against the West Indies (in the summer of 1991) and was then selected for the 1992 World Cup in Australia and New Zealand.

IT AIN'T OVER UNTIL THE FAT MAN SWINGS
*Newspaper headline after ITB had hit the winning runs against the West In the Fifth Test at the Oval, levelling the series at 2-2*

I fought hard to make sure that I got Ian Botham to the World Cup. The old lion had been a breath of fresh air during the Oval Test against the West Indies. He revelled in his comeback, practised seriously and keenly, jollied and jockeyed up the youngsters and put them on a keen Test match 'edge'. They relished his presence.
*Graham Gooch*

I told Micky Stewart he'd picked hassle.
*Peter May*

It was just one of those days when everything went my way. The pitch was a bit two-paced but most of their guys just holed out. I haven't done anything different – I'm still drinking as much.

*ITB after his one-man demolition of the Aussies in the World Cup*

Ian Botham provided the Aussies with the best excuse to gloss over their World Cup shortcomings... it was less painful to praise Botham than to criticise their own heroes.
*Graham Ottway, Today*

Kiwi Ump.
*ITB explains the reason for his dismissal for a duck in the 1992 World Cup final off a ball he claims never to have hit*

On returning from the World Cup, ITB joined his third and final county, Durham, who were about to embark on their inaugural season as a first-class county.

Had a pint of Castle Eden in the Dun Cow. Botham and Richards said they'd join us but disappeared into a back room of the pavilion, and locked the door. What were they doing? Your guess is as good as mine.
*Durham team mate Simon Hughes*

It was a bit sad in the end at Durham, seeing him bowl those diddly-doddlers and getting carted all over the ground.
*Graham Gooch*

Blimey, this man's arse is kissed, innit?
*Durham overseas star Dean Jones reacts to yet another batsman falling for the ITB long-hop*

Placard outside a cricket ground: The part of Ian Botham will be played by Derek Pringle.
*Cartoon in Private Eye alluding to ITB's dual career as pantomime King and occasional England cricketer*

Like me, he was totally brassed off and frustrated by the amount of tampering we had seen the Pakistanis do during the series, and also by the fact that we knew our Board knew but had not made any official objection. That is why 'Both' rang the press box to alert them.
*Allan Lamb*

John Arlott taught me everything I know about quality of life.
*ITB's tribute to the great writer and commentator*

Dear Mr Botham
We very much enjoyed the way you danced after taking a wicket in the World Cup '92. This letter is to ask if you would be interested in importing cashew nuts from factories here in Kerala... you might be able to set up a shop.
*One of the 15-odd letters received by ITB every day during his time at Durham*

## 1993: THE FINAL SEASON

At the beginning of the season, ITB declared his intention to retire – aged 37 – in September. However, after he failed to break into the England side, his increasingly injury-wracked body inspired him to quit suddenly halfway through the season.

If 'producing the goods', in terms of Test selection, is to take two for 29 and score 13 in a social fixture, heaven help us if Botham ever becomes chairman of selectors.
*Ted Dexter reacts to Botham's fury at not being considered for the Ashes series*

One morning last week it took me five minutes to get out of bed. I thought, I don't need this anymore. I've had 10 operations – back, shoulder, wrist, knee, cheek. I'm like an old battered old Escort; you might find one panel that's original.
*ITB blames declining fitness for his retirement*

Does Botham have the charm or perceptiveness to endure in the celebrity stakes as Henry Cooper and Geoff Boycott and David Gower and Gary Lineker are likely to.
*Colin Bateman worries about ITB's future*

Has there been a worse year for British sport?
*Independent sports editor Paul Newman linking ITB's retirement to the loss, in some form, of Brian Clough, Paul Gascoigne, James Hunt, Nigel Mansell, Booby Moore, David Platt and Peter Scudamore*

Durham county player Ian Botham retires today from first-class cricket, two months earlier than expected, at the end of this team's match against the Australians.
*The Financial Times gets over-excited*

I'm going top be the next British ambassador to Karachi.
*ITB's unlikely choice of a new career (turns out, he was only joking)*

No way England can save the series while Gooch continues as captain. With Gooch at the helm they look like a bunch of men condemned to walk up Tyburn Hill before being publicly hanged one after another.
*ITB*

I hope they don't win anything for 100 years.
*ITB, showing that he hadn't yet forgotten and forgiven Somerset's 'betrayal' of 1986*

There were nine young girls on the jury who didn't know the difference between a football and a cricket ball. We should have had a multi-racial jury, instead we had 11 English people. And most of those were women who kept looking and smiling at Lamby and Robin Smith and Botham. That's understandable. They are national heroes, but it was not a serious court case – that's why we stopped it.
*Pakistani pace bowler Sarfraz Nawaz on the decision to drop his libel case against Allan Lamb, who had accused him of ball tampering. ITB appeared as a defence witness.*

# 1994-1996

## THE ANTI-ESTABLISHMENT, WOULD-BE ESTABLISHMENT MAN

FOR MUCH OF THE TWO YEARS FOLLOWING HIS RETIREMENT, ITB did the rounds of press, TV and radio interviews promoting his autobiography. Like many former players, he also turned pundit as soon as he hung up his boots. But Beefy being Beefy that was never going to be enough.

Before too long his criticism of Ray Illingworth's reign as England manager and chairman of the selectors had turned into a fully fledged campaign to run English cricket. The takeover bid was launched in typical Botham style – no holds barred. The scourge of the establishment was not going to soften his style in his attempt to talk his way inside.

All in all ITB still dominated the cricketing headlines in much the same way as he had done in his playing pomp.

## 1994-1995

No I've told you, I'm Fanny Craddock now, you're Johnny.
*ITB to wife Kath as he cooks the 6lb sea bass he had just caught*

Beefy doesn't even eat red meat any more. 'I don't like the taste', he shrugs. Nor does he drink beer, 'Well, very rarely. I prefer wine, I've quite a collection actually. Standing at a bar drinking pints is too much like hard work'.
*Today*

People ask why I want to live on Alderney, but I love it. I hate cities. Jersey is too busy for me. After 20-odd years under the microscope, with my feet never touching the ground, it is good to come back here and switch off. And it is great for the kids. No crime, no violence, no perverts walking around. It's a great life.
*ITB*

She has already begun practising her nursing skills – on her dad. Ian has a phobia about needles and at first would leave the room when she was injecting herself. But one night we were out at a Chinese restaurant and he finally let her do a finger prick test on him, although he turned his head away.
*Kathy Botham on her daughter Becky's diabetes*

You have a friendship for life with people like that [England team-mates] – a bit like, I should think, the guys who used to stand next to each other in the trenches. It is a similar thing. They are fighting for their lives, we are playing for our livelihoods.
*ITB on how he misses comradeship of team-mates*

A *Question Of Sport* has been going for a quarter of a

century. Which century I'm not sure, but it feels like the 16th. They've tried to update Botham, Beaumont and Coleman by throwing away the Pringle sweaters but all it has done is change the collective smell of a musty uncle from Old Spice to Hai Karate. At least Botham has shed his long locks. But it has merely changed his image from a member of a Seventies pop group to a member of an over-seventies bowls team.
*Brian Reade*

Ian and I are old mates, but we aren't Morecambe and Wise.
*Bill Beaumont announces his and ITB's retirement from A Question of Sport*

I don't think I'll ever be good enough to make it to the Seniors' Pro Circuit. But I'd dearly love to be good enough to play county golf. I'm told that, as a tax exile based in Alderney, I could qualify for Hampshire. But the standard is so high, I'll have to knock seven shots off my handicap.
*ITB*

Not many amateurs hit the ball as far. I know how good he can be.
*Golfer Sam Torrance on ITB's golfing prowess*

I needed a break from cricket and it needed a break from me.
*ITB on his retirement*

At the Savoy last week to launch the paperback of his memoirs, Ian Botham talked of his affection for the late John Arlott, who let him in on the secrets of the vine. Arlott took 2,000 bottles to his retirement home on Alderney. The remains of the collection are for sale and Beefy plans to buy it. He needs a few good corks because, as a tribute, he likes to place one on Arlott's grave when he visits.
*Sunday Times*

It's a sad day for cricket. In a few years it has lost its two major voices, Brian and John Arlott. I think the testimonies show what we all thought of 'Johnners'. Players enjoyed their company. You can't say that about many commentators.
*ITB on the death of Brian Johnston*

From the moment Ian Botham's career started to wane, each new all-rounder England have tried has been under enormous pressure to fill the great man's boots. Many have tried and, for whatever reason, have simply not been up to the task. But I am in no doubt that Gough can be the answer to nation's prayers. In fact, I believe that he is already further advanced than Botham was at the same stage of his career.
*Dennis Lillee*

Don't call me the new Botham.
*Darren Gough*

It's been much tougher for Darren Gough coming into
the England side at an almost identical age to me, 23
against 22. I came into an England side that had
Dennis Amiss, Alan Knott, Derek Underwood, Mike
Brearley, Tony Greig and Bob Willis. Nobody was
shouting: 'Botham's going to be the saviour of English
cricket.' But they have hailed Gough that way.
*ITB*

A man more than worthy of finally filling my boots.
*ITB on Dominic Cork*

Who the hell does Brian Lara think he is? Cricket has
made him a superstar and he should never forget it. I
believe I'm well qualified to talk about the pressures
that can spring from being labelled a cricket star. One
day I was hailed as a conquering hero. The next the
critics wanted me banished to Siberia. I honestly don't
believe young Brian has endured anything like the
attention I got.
*ITB on Brian Lara, who was complaining of burn-out*

But it is Botham who is the real surprise. Not because
he is a brilliant commentator, he is not. But he
certainly has the potential to become a very good one.
Botham appears to have completely reinvented his
personality. Gone, let us hope forever, is the arrogance
and boorish belligerence that made him such a great
cricketer but a rather charmless broadcaster on *A
Question of Sport*. In its place is a quietly spoken,
thoughtful commentator anxious to share his interest-

ing views on the game. On second thoughts, it must be a different Ian Botham.
*The Times*

Newspapers have been full of pieces about how impressive Sky's coverage is and what an excellent commentator new boy Ian Botham is proving to be. Most of the stuff, it is true, had appeared in Murdoch papers under the usual back-scratch rules. An exception is a large piece in The Daily Telegraph extolling Botham's virtues at the microphone which was written by Mark Nicholas, Telegraph sports writer but also Sky commentator.
*Private Eye*

Presenter Charles Colvile is increasingly Alan Partridge for real, all gung ho chauvinism and shrieked excitement. The rest operate in a largely bewildering jock-speak. After one dismissal in the Second Test, Botham repeated three times the same comment, 'Bit of a haymaker, that shot... good catch, low down'.
*Private Eye*

Ian Botham was forced to miss an England match yesterday – or risk his status as cricket's first-ever tax exile. The millionaire sportsman had spent Wednesday commentating for Sky TV on England's one-day international against the West Indies. But bad weather forced the match into a second day. Botham, who still owns a farmhouse in North Yorkshire,

spends most of his time living in a three-bedroomed fisherman's cottage on Alderney in the Channel Islands. But under strict tax rules he can only retain his 'exile' status if he spends no more than 62 days in Britain. When England failed to wrap up the match against the Windies, Botham was faced with his taxing problem. If he had not left Britain by midnight on Wednesday he would have wasted one of his precious days in the country.
*Daily Mirror*

Ian Botham revealed today that he wants to get back into top flight cricket in an official capacity – either selecting, coaching or motivating the national side. Botham believes Ray Illingworth is too old to be chairman of selectors and that English cricket is 'again run by amateurs and played by professionals'. He claims: 'Why should it be the case that you have to be in your 60s before you're even considered for a position of power and authority in the game.'
*The Daily Telegraph*

Ian Botham has begun serious negotiations to become Sri Lanka's cricket supremo. Anura Tennekoon, secretary of the Sri Lankan Board said: 'We believe that Botham has all the attributes necessary to give our players the benefit of his vast experience and knowledge in Test cricket. Botham said: 'Let's face it, if I can't do a better job for Sri Lanka than Ray Illingworth is doing for England then something is very wrong. Why am I interested in this job? I'm keen

because I'm 20 years too young to be considered for a responsible job in the game here.'
*Mail on Sunday*

I don't agree with everything that Ray Illingworth says but now that he's got the power, we've got to let him get on with it and give him the chance to show what can be done.
*ITB on England's new manager*

Illingworth is clueless about the demands of modern cricket. He would have been the right man 10, 15 or 20 years ago.
*ITB a month later*

Illy's not a motivator, he's a whinger.
*ITB*

Botham already has one revolutionary idea for discussion. He wants to change the law governing bowlers running on the pitch after delivering the ball. Presently, bowlers are only allowed to land on the pitch in line with the stumps within four feet of the popping crease. Botham wants that area extended to five and a half feet, saying: 'It would help spinners by providing them with a bit of broken ground to turn the ball out of which is not, as now, merely on the length of a half-volley. Secondly, by enabling pacemen to bowl from closer to the line of the stumps, it will help them move the ball into, and most importantly, away from the bat from a much straighter line. All of which would go some way to redressing the current imbalance in favour of batsmen.

*Peter Hayter reports on ITB's nomination for the MCC's cricket committee*

## 1996

If I had my way, I'd take Ray Illingworth to Traitor's Gate and personally hang, draw and quarter him.

*ITB*

English cricket is crying out for someone like Botham to take charge. Ray Illingworth has this iron-fisted way of ruling and it cannot get the best out of the different characters in a team. If you were five minutes late for a net when Both was in command, it would not become a big disciplinary issue. Both would put his arm around you and say 'I hope she was worth it' or 'it must have been a heavy night'. He would have a crack about it then get down to work.

*Wayne Larkins*

I feel very upset for the wives, girlfriends and families. I cannot imagine how they must have felt when they arrived back at Heathrow to discover that they had been blamed by Ray Illingworth for England losing the series. Even to make such a suggestion is completely out of order. It just seems to me that the families are an easy scapegoat for the manager to point the finger at.

*Kathy Botham joins the attack on Illy after England return home having lost the Test series against South Africa 1-0*

Some might say Ian is just a talented thug but I believe there is far more to him than that. The fact is that he is our most distinguished cricketer of recent times, if not of all time, and we must try and harness his talents. In the right frame of mind Ian would be a superb motivator. Just remember what effect his self-belief had on the Australians, for instance. Very often they went weak at the knees when he was around. I recall the World Cup match against them in Sydney when they simply couldn't live with his sheer presence. Imagine what impact he might have if he was able to inspire others the way he could inspire himself.
*Test and County Cricket Board chairman Dennis Silk*

I'd like to hear what Dennis has to say and I would be keen to help in any way I can. How good am I as a motivator? I could sell ice to the Eskimos.
*ITB*

Ian Botham is the choice of senior England players to succeed Ray Illingworth as manager after the World Cup. One source close to the England camp said last night: 'The players want him because he's great in the dressing room. He's brilliant at getting players going and giving them confidence'.
*The Daily Mail*

I never thought I would say this but, for the future of English cricket, it would be best if our World Cup stays a miserable disaster. Only then will the real

failures responsible for throwing our game into a self-destructing tailspin finally wake up. I'm talking about the secretaries and chairmen of the counties. They can be found in their committee rooms, glasses in hand, fooling themselves that everything in the garden is rosy. Well it isn't. And unless we get wise we are going to end up playing the Eskimos. And losing.
*ITB*

I can see Ian Botham performing a very important role in the dressing-room in a coaching and motivational capacity. He clearly gets on well with the players and I think this England team needs as many people to help it as possible.
*David Graveney, would-be chairman of selectors*

In March 1996, ITB had a real chance to get his hands on some power. A new selection panel was to be chosen. ITB was nominated along with eight others. Opinion on the wisdom of appointing him a selector was fiercely divided.

I would love to serve on the selection panel because the biggest challenge now is to turn England into a world power again. I have never been more serious about anything in my life.
*ITB*

Personally, I think it would be a complete waste for him just to be a rank-and-file selector.
*David Gower backs ITB for the top job*

What matters is the things I would offer, like motivation, encouragement and self-belief. I played with most of these guys, so they trust me. We have the same humour, play the same modern game. I can relate to what they are going through.
*ITB*

I get phone calls, I get messages saying 'Please give me a ring'. It happens all the time with players asking me to speak to them or come to watch them.
*ITB who claims to have been helping certain England players for five years*

Move over Ray Illingworth – the people want Ian Botham to plot England's Test fortunes NOW! An overwhelming 88 per cent of Mirror readers want our greatest Test all-rounder to take over the reins.
*Daily Mirror*

Let's get the old farts out, the people's choice in and get back to the top of world cricket. – *Major (retd) DG Wood*
Don't give up on Botham – we need him. He's popular with the normal people of this country – *Maggie Edwards and the staff of Alpha Insurance, Gillingham*
Every ten minutes the whole office chants 'There's only one Beefy Botham'. For God's sake get him in – *The Business to Business office, Birmingham*
I don't know one end of a cricket bat from another, but I do know Botham is the man for the job – *Brenda Coles*

Before we get too carried away with nostalgia, let's
not forget Botham was the worst captain England ever
had – *P Rowlands*
Why does Ian Botham want to be on the selection
committee? When he is on *A Question of Sport* he
always groans when he is asked a cricket question –
*Mrs Pickles*
*Letters to the Daily Mirror*

Ray Illingworth last night offered Ian Botham an olive
branch when he said: 'I'd work with him provided
I'm in charge and have the final say on selection.'
*Daily Mirror*

If this had been Australia, Botham would be an
automatic choice as a selector. We held the man in
awe over here. I can only believe that they are scared
of him. He is a rebel and can be a bit intimidating, but
so what. The pride and the passion has been missing
from English cricket and Botham is just the man to
put it back.
*Allan Border*

I do not think we want a high profile selector roaring
around the place. You don't need jollity between
players and selectors. We need wise counsel in the
background. Look at the Australians. I don't think
anyone knows who their selectors are. It's certainly
not Allan Border or Dennis Lillee.
*Ted Dexter*

There is still a fear of me, a near paranoia in some places.
*ITB*

Botham sees himself becoming the great unifying force in English cricket. A look at his curriculum vitae, however, reveals a great talent: not for unification, but for division. You are either on the bus or off the bus, that was always the unspoken team motto and Beefy was always the driver. He has always created a team within a team. There were Beefy's good ol' boys and those outsiders. Anyone not prepared to be one of Beefy's courtiers were bores, straight and poofs.
*Simon Barnes*

Botham's idea of team spirit was to squirt a water pistol at someone and then go off and get pissed. There's a bit more to it than that.
*Ray Illingworth*

For him to stand as a selector is ridiculous because you're meant to watch cricket for 90 days a year and I don't think Botham's allowed into the country for more than 75.
*Chris Cowdrey points out an obvious problem with tax exile ITB becoming a selector*

There is an air of desperation about the Wot We Want is Beefy brigade, as if all the ills of English cricket can be solved at one fell swoop simply by drafting our greatest all-rounder (retd) onto the Test selection

panel. This is not 1981. Botham cannot stride Lancelot-like from the pavilion with bat-twirling or charge in from the gasworks end like Jonah Lomu on acid to single-handedly compensate for the collective inadequacies of others. Botham would be no better than Illingworth and has demonstrated a siege mentality in the past, bordering on the paranoid, which would soon permeate the dressing room.
*Richard Littlejohn*

I wouldn't have Botham as manager. To be in the position of England manager you've got to earn someone's respect. I can't see a bloke like him earning too many people's respect. I lost my respect for him very early. How can you respect a guy who puts an empty beer glass in your face and says he will cut you from ear to ear. How can you respect someone like that? England manager? Don't make me laugh. I wouldn't have him fixing my door. I have no respect from him as a human being. The only thing he could teach the England team is how to roll a spliff.
*Ian Chappell, obviously still sore about his run-in with a young Botham in Melbourne during the mid-seventies*

I have never threatened to cut anyone from ear to ear with a bottle, glass, razor blade, pork pie or feather duster. If anyone seriously alleges that I have threatened to slit their throats, then I will see them in court.
*ITB's reply*

Despite his grass roots support, ITB was considered too much of a wild card by the county chairmen, whose votes decide the make up of the selection committee. Almost immediately a new debate began over whether ITB should be involved in a coaching capacity with the English team.

When riches were spread in front of me to tempt me away to South Africa, I always said no. But Gooch took the money. I can't pretend it doesn't hurt to be beaten by someone who didn't always put his country first.
*ITB reacts to the news that he has been beaten in the selector election by Graham Gooch*

Botham is England through and through. He had a never-say-die attitude, won games on his own. Ian's a terrific age, I find him great company. I'm sure he will have something to give England in the future.
*England coach David Lloyd*

We will not be using Ian Botham in any capacity with the England team. Our new coach David Lloyd has his own personality and he needs time to get used to his job. Having Botham around would just get in the way. We all know that Botham could motivate himself, but he could never manage to motivate anybody else as captain. We have discussed a possible role for Botham but he has been in print in the last couple of days and it hasn't done him any good.
*Ray Illingworth*

The only man that Ian Botham can motivate is himself.
*Alec Bedser, the man who, as chairman of selectors, appointed ITB to his brief and disastrous spell as captain*

Ian Botham, it seems, can't be given a role in coaching the England Test team because, according to Ray Illingworth, 'We don't know how good he is at motivating others'. This seems a little odd given that a whole generation of youth became motivated to participate in cricket because of Botham, whereas I'm not sure how many schoolkids have ever said, 'When I grow up I want to be Ray Illingworth'.
*Mark Steel*

Botham must stick with it. It is absolutely essential that we get people of his quality back on the scene. I am delighted to read that he intends hammering away at the door until someone hears him. We seem to be getting carried away with the media clash. The problem is that every England captain and any top cricketer worth his salt and with strong views on the game is in demand by newspapers and television.
*Bob Willis on suggestions that ITB would have to drop his media work to be involved with the England team*

Botham was very keen on coming. It would have done Glamorgan a power of good and given him a firm base for his England ambitions.
*The Daily Mail on Botham for Glamorgan*

## BOTHAM V IMRAN

In the summer of 1996, ITB and Allan Lamb took the former Pakistani cricket captain Imran Khan to court for libel. Their action was based on two quotes attributed to Imran during the debate over ball-tampering allegations levelled at the Pakistani cricket team. The first was widely used in the British press, the second came from an Indian news magazine, India Today.

The biggest names in English cricket have all done it.
*Imran Khan on ball tampering*

There is a lot of racism in this society. Look at people like Lamb and Botham making statements like, 'Oh, I never thought much of him anyway, and now its been proved he's a cheat'. Look at Tony Lewis, Christopher Martin-Jenkins, Derek Pringle. They are all educated Oxbridge types. Look at the others. Lamb, Botham, Trueman. The difference in class and upbringing makes a difference.
*Imran Khan (allegedly) draws a distinction between those he thought had taken a 'reasonable' view of the ball-tampering debate (Lewis, CMJ and Pringle) and those whose criticism of the Pakistani team he claimed was based on racism and ignorance (Lamb, Botham and Trueman)*

Imran argued that the first quote did not refer specifically to ITB, although he did attempt to prove that the Englishman was a ball-tamperer in court, before withdrawing the allegation after ITB denied it in the witness box. As for the 'upbringing' quote, Imran simply claimed he had been misquoted.

Both ITB and Imran employed high ranking barristers to plead their case and for a few weeks the High Court in London was thronged with famous cricketers called to give their testimony. Imran Khan's QC, George Carman, decided to undermine ITB's case by bringing up his past misdemeanours. ITB's response to this line of questioning, as you'd expect, was robust.

All wide ties and short skirts.
*The Sunday Telegraph on the appearance of Lamb, ITB and their wives*

Looking as though they dropped in from Planet Vogue.
*The Sunday Telegraph on Imran and his wife Jemima (nee Goldsmith)*

I come from a working middle-class background.
*ITB*

I thought the days of the amateurs versus the professional sportsmen were long gone.
*ITB on Imran's class slur*

I'd like to inform Imran that my wife and I have a very successful marriage, thank you.
*ITB responding to Imran's comment on ITB's autobiography, 'The real hero of the book is Botham's wife, Kathy. I wish her all the luck for the remainder of her marriage.'*

0.19 grammes. I remember it well.
*ITB on the drugs raid on his house*

You tend to panic when faced with journalists, sir.
*ITB, when accused of lying by George Carman*

He's from Australia. I didn't take any notice.
*ITB's explanation of his failure to sue Ian Chappell who
called him a habitual liar*

I like to think I could touch down anywhere in the
world and knock on someone's door and, whatever
creed or nationality, they would be pleased to see me.
*ITB rejecting charges of racism*

There aren't too many places I can wander into
around the world and womanise. I'm often recognised
in seconds.
*ITB pouring scorn on the Miss Barbados allegations*

There's only one woman in my life, and that's Kath.
She's like a good claret, the older she gets, the better
she get.
*ITB*

If I'd slept with all the women I'm supposed to have
done, all  I can say is, 'Erroll Flynn eat your heart out'.
*ITB*

You can stretch the laws to a point. You can nick it or
you can walk. If  you're  playing against the
Australians you don't walk.
*ITB*

What nails? I've bitten my nails since I was a kid.
*ITB on George Carman's accusation that he gouged the ball
with his thumbnails*

I used to say that whenever the camera panned in on
him on the field of play, he was either picking his nose
or chewing his nails. He would do it so much they
would bleed.
*Kathy Botham*

Sometimes when you have had a barrel of port it can
be difficult.
*ITB when asked if it gets more difficult to swing the ball as
you get older*

You never stop learning in cricket. I'm sure that in ten
years time they'll find another way of swinging the
ball.
*ITB*

Cricket balls don't swing like they used to. They
changed the centre of the ball in the late 1970s and
early 1980s. The ball has never swung as much since,
legally, at least.
*ITB*

It was part of the game. It was an habitual thing.
When bowlers held the ball they automatically tampered with the seam. I would disagree with that practice and I never saw Ian Botham tamper with the ball.
*Former England wicket-keeper Bob Taylor*

Revenge was sought for the inglorious England defeat of 1992. The knives were out and Allan Lamb and Ian Botham, for their own reasons, were prepared to join the attack on Imran Kahn and reject the olive branch of friendship.
*Imran's QC George Carman on why ITB and Lamb had brought the case*

From 1981 onwards, he began to lose that outswing and gradually his performances started going down.
*Imran's explanation of why his claim that the greatest bowlers tampered with the ball did not libel ITB*

His autobiography should have been called Rambotham.
*Imran reflecting on Botham's account of an Indiana Jones style tour to Pakistan*

I tried everything, short of humiliating myself and lying so that I could apologise. Then I started to realise that the plaintiffs did not want to settle. Probably they just wanted me to be humiliated.
*Imran Khan*

In the interests of the great name of cricket, and to avoid a blood battle in the courts and in the interests of good relations between the Pakistan cricket team and the English cricket team, did you not think that it was a fair and reasonable proposal which you might accept?
*Carman to ITB on Imran's proposal to write a letter to The Times declaring he thought neither Lamb or ITB were*

*cheats or racists*

No sir. I did not accept it as an apology.
*ITB's reply*

Much to ITB's shock, the jury found against Botham and Lamb, landing them with a legal bill of around £500,000.

I'm a little confused as to how it went against us.  If you had been in there for two-and-a half weeks, then I think it is a conclusion you are entitled to come to.
*ITB*

Ian Botham and Allan Lamb weren't the only two people to be taken by surprise by the jury's verdict in the Imran Khan libel trial. BBC Radio were so sure that Imran would be found guilty, that they only bothered to prepare a report announcing this outcome. The jury's 'unexpected' verdict was the signal for some frantic rewriting.
*Inside Edge*

There was one other striking feature of this trial. Every observer regarded it as a petty argument that had got out of control, that could and should have been settled with an apology and a handshake. The jury's message seemed to be that they thought their time had been wasted. And it is hard to quarrel with that.
*Matthew Engel*

Much was made in the press of Imran's abandonment, mid-way through the trial, of his plea of 'justification' (i.e. that what had been said was true). Imran's argument, from the beginning, had been that much of what is called 'ball tampering' is not cheating and should not be illegal. He introduced video evidence of Botham prodding the ball with his fingers, not to prove the England all-rounder was a 'cheat', but in support of his contention that 'ball-tampering' was widespread. When Botham protested that his actions were perfectly legitimate, it was logical for Imran to accept him at his word – since that was all he was asking of Botham in return [i.e. that he had never accused ITB of being a cheat or a racist]. Much of the media may have had difficulty in grasping this elementary point, but the jury did not.

*Mike Marqusee*

# TABLOID HELL

ITB HAD THE MISFORTUNE TO BECOME CRICKET'S FIRST household name since Denis Compton in the middle of one of the fiercest circulation battles ever known in the British press.

The UK's tabloid newspapers – notably, but not only, The *Sun* and the *News of the World* – identified a handful of national figures with which to wage their sales war. These included Prince Charles and Princess Diana, Boy George and one sportsman... Ian Botham.

With each the formula was the same, build them up – often relying on the target's ever-inflating ego to help in this process – and then chart the seemingly inevitable fall from grace once the media spotlight began to pick out their imperfections.

To give the stories the widest possible appeal, the coverage concentrated on the personal, rather than the public, aspects of their lives. Sex was the biggest seller, followed by drug abuse.

Once ITB was elevated to the status of a tabloid love/hate figure, he could never escape it. From 1984 onwards, scandal followed scandal. The slightest slip – a bar room brawl or a night of overindulgence – could be splashed on the front page because it concerned a tabloid 'star' and was therefore automatically 'news'.

Often the stories were completely untrue – such as the allegation that ITB head-butted a hotel porter in 1988 – and in nearly all cases they were hugely exaggerated. But whatever their merits as pieces of journalism – ITB admits that he was no monk during his cricket career – the stories were still read by tens of millions of people. Because of this their impact on ITB himself and English cricket in general was often earth-shattering.

If only a quarter of the things written about me were true. I'd be completely pickled by now and would have sired half the children in the world.
*ITB*

I don't think the headlines are quite finished. In the past I've thought: 'They can't get any worse' and I've been proved wrong.
*Kathy Botham in 1988*

A tabloid editor can never have enough scandals. You can save them up for lean spells and the run-up to elections or push them out if your rivals come up with a real beauty to lure back readers. What Ian Botham did was to make cricket a subject from which the press would try to squeeze scandal. As a result, off-the-field antics – the kind which tabloid hacks have a knack for tracking down – are now seen as causing poor on-field performances, even as grounds for ending a career. Did Mike Gatting wind up losing his job

as England captain because Ian Botham had attracted
the flies?
*Philip Cornwall*

The central cricketing figure behind this increased
interest in cricket by news editors was Ian Botham.
His rise to glory in the late 1970s and early 1980s
coincided with an era in which the expectations and
importance of national teams were exaggerated
because of England's inability to come to terms with
its own mediocrity as a world power. Before Botham,
cricketers were generally left alone by the tabloid
press. After Botham, cricket could never be free of
them. As major stories go, he was, in Graham Gooch's
words, 'a godsend', for the press. Loud, opinionated
and a bit of a carouser, Botham provided English
cricket and the national press with something they
sorely lacked: a winner.
*Jim Melly*

The jealousy from tabloid hacks towards Botham was
quite incredible. It's so much part of this country's
nature to love putting people down.
*Rob Steen*

The other tabloids found it hard to forgive Botham his
exclusive and enriching relationship with The Sun.
They were out to get him.
*Peter Roebuck. ITB signed a deal early in his career to
'write' for The Sun*

## 1981

MY HELL, BY CLEARED BOTHAM

I was the most relieved man in Britain yesterday after a judge cleared me of assault. When Judge Richard Hutchinson announced that I was not guilty, I knew that my summer of secret hell was over at last. The allegation that I had kicked and punched 20 year-old sailor Steven Isbister hung over me like a shadow all through the cricket season and the Test matches against Australia.

*ITB in The Sun*

There must be one law for England cricketers and another law for the rest of us.

*Labour MP Dennis Canavan protests to Attorney-General Sir Michael Havers on hearing that the Police had decided that 'because of Botham's importance' the decision to bring charges must 'come from the top'*

A loads of codswallop from a parcel of rogues.

*ITB's counsel Andrew Rawley QC on the allegations*

I didn't have the energy.

*ITB asked if he hit Steve Isbister*

I'd rather face Dennis Lillee with a stick of rhubarb than go through all that again.

*ITB*

## 1983

BOTHAM FINED FOR TELLING US THE TRUTH

Ian Botham has been fined £200 for speaking the truth. The Sun has been castigated for reporting it. The fine was imposed by tour manager Doug Insole as a punishment for Botham's remarks about the Australian umpires in last week's Test.
*The Sun*

## 1984

BOTHAM NAMED IN DRUGS SENSATION
I saw him spaced out in hotel, claims girl witness

Disturbing evidence has emerged that Ian Botham was smoking marijuana and had access to cocaine during the England cricket tour to New Zealand.

Magazine writer Mary Burgess went to the [hotel] room with a short, dark-haired Englishman – who gave his name only as 'Dickie Dirt' and saw Botham watching television. After talking to Botham about football Miss Burgess sat next to him, looked into his eyes and saw that he was 'spaced out'.

Then she heard a conversation in which Dickie Dirt asked Botham where the 'dope' was. Botham said there was not enough and then 'there's coke in the bag'. Dickie Dirt eventually came out of the bathroom with a little brown bottle and Botham said as Dickie Dirt emptied it onto his hand: 'Take it easy. It's uncut. It's pretty strong'.

Our reporters approached Botham in his room in the Hilton Hotel, Lahore [The England tour party had flown to Pakistan for the second Test series of the 1983-84 season]. Botham said of the allegations, from his bed where he was reading a book: 'We have heard all about it. We found it quite amusing. We will be able to retire after you have printed that, pal.'

England team manager Allan Smith said: 'The whole thing is a tissue of lies, misunderstandings and misidentification. I am getting fed up with the harassment of my players. If I get any more reports I will lay a complaint of harassment to the police. I am sure you do not want to spend two or three days in a Pakistani prison.'

In New Zealand a senior cricket official said: 'The Mail on Sunday's information is amazingly accurate. There is certainly a drugs problem with some members of the England team.'

There has also been a strong rumour in New Zealand that during the Saturday of the Second Test the England dressing room was 'like an opium den'.
*Mail on Sunday, 11 March*


BOTHAM FURY AT 'LUDICROUS ATTACK ON US'
England's cricket tour was a shambles last night amid more astonishing claims of drug taking, boozing and womanising. The latest bombshell came from a 24 year-old girl magazine reporter who insisted in a sworn statement that one player has been associated with drugs. Botham slammed the drugs allegations last night. 'To say the England team are drug addicts, or whatever way you want to put it, is totally ludicrous', he said.
*News of the World, 11 March*


BOTHAM FACES DRUGS PROBE BY POLICE

The New Zealand police yesterday began an investigation after receiving a dossier about the England players' off-the-field activities. Commissioner Ken Thompson said there would be 'vigorous inquiries'. 'I was shocked and amazed by the suggestions that I had been smoking pot', Botham said, 'I have never smoked pot in my life and as for cocaine I wouldn't even know what coke looked like. I thought the allegations were an early April Fool's joke'.
*Daily Mail, 12 March*

## LIES BLOODY LIES
Fly-home Botham's fury at drug 'smear'

Botham said: 'Why is it that I'm always the guy they want to knock? The big man they want to bring down? This time they have gone too far. This is the point where I show my strength – and I'll show it in the courts'.
*The Sun, 12 March*

## I'M NO JUNKIE SAYS BOTHAM
Injured star flies home to storm over 'drugs, birds and booze' tour

Cricket star Ian Botham flew home yesterday and angrily declared: 'All the allegations are utterly false. The only drug I take is for my asthma. As for being legless – that's a joke – I enjoy a pint, but is that a crime? To say we were drunk and fooling around with girls is nonsense'.
*Daily Star, 12 March*

What a shame English cricket is going to pot and isn't it a coincidence that it is Coke who are sponsoring the Pakistani team in this Test series?
*ITB keeps joking*

PLAYERS 'KEPT A SCORE BOARD OF SEX'
New allegations about the off-pitch antics of the England cricket team emerged yesterday. It is claimed [by New Zealand sports paper *Eight O'clock*] that although their performances were a disaster their night-time attempts to 'bowl a maiden over' were phenomenal. Some players, it was alleged, compiled a 'naughty scoreboard' to record their successes. A team member's 'batting average' depended on how much he had to spend on wining and dining a girl to get her into bed.
*Daily Star, 12 March*

He doesn't smoke pot.
*Elton John defends ITB, 14 March*

MY SECRET LOVE PACT WITH IAN
Bothams tell of 'strange marriage'

Cricket superstar Ian Botham's wife Kathy told yesterday how she managed to stay clam when her husband was branded a drug taker. The couple have a secret love pact. SHE ignores everything she hears or reads about Ian unless HE tells her himself.

[Ian said] 'Only the other day a woman wrote and offered me £100,000 if I would go off with her 21 year-old daughter. But it never enters Kathy's head to take any of these things seriously.'

When they go out together Kathy always walks a few paces ahead so people won't know she's his wife. This interview was the first she had ever given to a newspaper. 'I prefer it that way,' Kathy explained, 'I'm a very private person.'

[Ian said] 'Everyone thinks cricket is my first love but it comes second to Kath and the children. I don't give a damn what they say about my high jinks. There are only four women in my life – Kath, my little daughter Sarah and my two bitch dogs at home. If Raquel Welch walked in at this moment I wouldn't even give her the time of day.'
*News of the World, 18 March*

## BOTHAM ACCUSED BY TEST RIVAL IN NEW POT STORM

Pakistan's veteran fast bowler Sarfraz Nawaz claims Botham played cricket under the influence of drugs. He says in an article appearing in today's *Pakistan Times* that Botham was supplied with hash during the First Test in Karachi. Said Sarfraz: 'How could he perform well when he was drugged most of the time?'.
*Daily Express, 19 March*

## 1985

### VILLAGE HUNTS BOTHAM SNOUT

Neighbours of cricket star Ian Botham vowed yesterday to track down the informer who tipped off the police about cannabis hidden in a drawer at Botham's home. Butcher Don Stewart said: 'Whoever it was had

better watch out because feelings are running pretty high.'
*News of the World, February*

## BOTHAM FACES THREAT OF BAN

Lord's could take steps tomorrow to have Ian Botham banned from cricket. Lancashire chairman Cedric Rhoades is demanding action from the Test and County Cricket Board after Botham's £100 fine last month for possessing drugs.
*The Sun, 7 March*

## RAPPED BOTHAM IS STILL SKIPPER

Ian Botham last night got the all-clear to carry on as Somerset skipper – but was severely reprimanded by the county's cricket committee over his recent drugs conviction. Botham, who last week was also cleared by the TCCB to play on for England against Australia this summer, admitted: 'I regret very much being involved with cannabis briefly some three years ago and realise how wrong it was. I am totally opposed to the use of drugs by any sportsmen'.
*The Sun, 19 March*

## BOTHAM'S BACK ON THE GRASS AGAIN

*Rejected advertisement for Nike trainers reported by the Sun, 28 May*

## BOTHAM THE DEER HUNTER IN RUMPUS

Cricket star Ian Botham set out yesterday on an 880-mile charity walk – and marched straight into a row

with animal lovers. The beefy Test star came under fire after revealing that he has spent the last week shooting deer on a hunting trip. Richard Course, director of the League Against Cruel Sports said: 'I saw Mr Botham on TV on his charity walk but I think he was walking in the wrong direction. He should have walked into the sea and saved the wild life of Scotland'.
*News of the World, October*

BOTHAM AND PC 'IN DUST UP'
Cricket superstar Ian Botham punched a policeman three times during his cross-Britain charity walk, it was claimed yesterday. But last night Botham, who expects to finish his 880-mile walk for Leukemia research today, insisted: 'I didn't punch the policeman – I only pushed him'.
*The Sun, November*

I don't want to take the matter any further because I am a big supporter of the cause Ian Botham is championing.
*PC Peter Fleming, thumped by Botham on the John O' Groats to Lands End walk*

## 1986

BOTHAM DRUGS SHOCK
I'm aware that he smokes dope, but doesn't every-body.
*Tim Hudson in The Daily Star, 2 April*

TEST ACE IN SEX AND DRUGS SCANDAL
We have sworn affidavits from witnesses – including
some who admit to supplying Botham with drugs.
And we have tape recordings – including some made
secretly by investigators – in which witnesses confessed to involvement in drugs with the sporting hero.
We even have evidence that Botham has been caught
up in a globetrotting marathon of drug taking
covering New Zealand, Fiji, California the Caribbean
and Britain since 1984.

POT SMOKING BOTHAM HAS TRIP IN ROLLER
Ian Botham and his flamboyant millionaire manager
Tim Hudson had a high old time smoking pot
together in Hudson's swanky Rolls-Royce.
*News of the World, 6 April*

LINDY AND ME
Botham talks about island blonde

Ian Botham talked yesterday about the stunning
blonde who claims she was involved in cocaine and
sex romps with the England cricket star in Barbados.
He admitted he had met former Miss World
contestant Lindy Field, but said her story about frolics
was ridiculous.
*Daily Star, 7 April*

THEY CAN'T BREAK OUR LOVE
Cricket superstar Ian Botham's pretty wife Kathy
yesterday bravely brushed aside the sex-and-drugs
scandal surrounding her husband. She told *The Sun*.

'My love for him and his love for me is so strong, nothing can harm it. The people who are saying these things can go on as much as they want but they won't break the special marriage and friendship we have'.
*The Sun, 7 April*

[ITB said] 'For two years, I have been hounded by people having a go at me about talking drugs. How on earth could I play international cricket if I was taking drugs. Nothing could be more ridiculous than suggestions I was standing in the slips in a Test match with cocaine in my flannels'.
*ITB quoted in The Sun, 7 April*

I would like to think I have better taste than that.
*ITB asked by the BBC's Frank Bough if he'd slept with Lindy Field, 7 April*

I am very much a man's man. I enjoy a few beers with the lads and by the time you leave at 10 or 11 o'clock, especially in this heat, you have got to get your sleep.
*ITB*

BOTHAM ROW GIRL SAYS SORRY
Former beauty queen Lindy Field yesterday apologised over the sex-and-drugs claims that have rocked cricket star Ian Botham's career. The one-time Miss World contestant said she was 'very sorry' for the hurt her allegations had caused the Botham family. But she stood by her allegations.
*Daily Express, 8 April*

I SAW IAN BOTHAM TAKE HEROIN
He begged for drugs in a 2am phone call

Wild man of cricket Ian Botham took the killer drug heroin while touring New Zealand with the England team in 1984. Raven-haired Vivien Kinsella – a self confessed drug addict – gave him a fix after he phoned her at 2 am and asked 'Have you got any drugs? I'm dry'.
*News of the World, 20 April*

BOTHAM: I DID TAKE POT
Exclusive: England cricket star confesses

'The fact is that I have, at various times in the past, smoked pot. I had been with a group of people who had been doing it and I went along with it. On other occasions I have smoked simply in order to relax – to get off the sometimes fearful treadmill of being an international celebrity, trying to forget for a moment the pressures which were on me all the time'.
*The Mail on Sunday, 18 May*

## 1987

Hell-raising Ian Botham was involved in an amazing sex act with a semi-naked girl at a wild cricket rave up in Sydney. Cheering partygoers, some high on cocaine, roared their approval as the stunning brunette removed Botham's trousers and stripped off most off her clothes. Then to wild applause... she performed a sex act on him.
*The People*

## 1988

BOOZED-UP BOTHAM WRECKED OUR CLUB!
Ian Botham was plunged into a new storm last night
after a massive booze up with Dennis Lillee. England
superstar Botham and veteran Aussie pace hero Lillee
have been accused of throwing and smashing glasses
as they took part in a rowdy drinking contest.
*The Sun, March*

An average boozing session at Taunton's Gardeners'
Arms meant sinking TEN pints of the landlord's
strongest lager PLUS ten DOUBLE gin and tonics.
*The Sun reports on ITB's alleged drinking habits as a
youngster, June*

BOOZED BOTHAM NUTTED HOTEL GUARD
*The Sun, December*

## 1989

BOTHAM BANNED FOR DOING 107MPH
Cricket superstar Ian Botham was banned from driving yesterday for doing 107mph – then said: 'I
deserve it'. Police caught him on the M42 as he
zoomed to a business meeting in his Ford Granada
Scorpio.
*The Sun, February*

## 1991

BED BUSTER BOTHAM'S TELLY ROMP
ITV is to make a musical based on cricketer Ian
Botham's reported BONKING exploits. The £1m romp

– Caught Behind – is loosely based on the England 1986 West Indies tour. London Weekend light entertainment chief John Kaye Cooper said: 'We've tried to combine sex, cricket and royalty. Former Monty Python star Eric Idle wrote the words. The music is by Teenage Mutant Ninja Turtle film composer John Du Prez.
*The Sun, May*

I DIDN'T WANT TO HURT BOTHAM
Confessions of his kiss 'n' tell beauty queen

I had no intention of talking about Botham. I really liked the guy. I want my son to grow up looking up to Ian Botham as his hero.
*Daily Star, August*

## 1994

I'LL SUE BOTHAMS FOR SEX AND DRUGS SLUR
The passionate beauty who broke the bed with Ian Botham was last night planning to put the star through another earth-shattering experience – by taking him to court for branding her a liar. Lindy Field is furious the ex-England cricketer is slamming her claims that they had a fling in a new book.

Lindy Field said: 'I gather Botham's book is called Don't Tell Kath. It should be WAKE UP Kath.' [She added]: 'I told Ian I couldn't see him one night. What I didn't tell him was that I was going out with Bungalow Bill Wiggins – who was also going out with Joan Collins. Actor Eric Idle [also] knew of my affair [with Botham]'.
*News of the World, September*

## 1995

A beauty branded a liar by cricketer Ian Botham after claims of a sex fling has come up on the Lottery – and says 'Now I may sue him'. Lindy Field – who scooped £216,000 said: 'I could still sue Ian Botham. He deserves to be sued. He needs shutting up because he talks rubbish. You can't print what I think of him'.
*The Daily Star, 12 July*

The rafters of Ian Botham's house in Ravensworth, North Yorkshire, will rock this weekend as he hosts his 40th birthday party. But why hasn't he invited his most loyal friend? For some reason Beefy seems to have forgotten Andy Withers, the famous minder who did everything from iron Ian's cricket whites to protect him from belligerent bruisers at the bars the cricketer used to frequent. A close friend of Ian's tells me: 'This guy really knows where all the bodies are buried. He was offered mega-money to spill the beans when he and Ian went their separate ways, but Andy never once opened his mouth'. There are those who say Ian's autobiography told a partial truth about his glory years as England's great all-rounder. Any book by Andy Withers – who now drives cabs for a living – might just fill in the tantalising gaps. Not too late to send off that invite, Beefy.
*Today, 28 September*

DEATH THREAT TO BOTHAM
The knives – and even the guns – will be out for cricket superstar Ian Botham when he goes to

Pakistan next February to commentate on the World Cup for Sky TV. 'He will have to be very, very careful', a journalist from Karachi told me. 'If he goes out on his own, or has too much to drink and starts shooting his mouth off, he could be in serious danger'. It's not so much Botham's juvenile off-the-cuff remark about sending your mother-in-law to Pakistan for a holiday that has upset the Pakistanis so much. It's more to do with his libel lawsuit against former Pakistan captain Imran Khan.
*Sunday Mirror*

## 1996

OWZAT FOR A PERFECT MATCH BEEFY?
Botham's first novel is about a boozy cricket romeo who loves playing the fool. Sounds familiar, doesn't it?

England's finest cricket hero sprawls in his car in a drunken stupor, his trousers round his ankles. In his lap a stunning blonde, naked apart form a pair of pads and a cricket cap. It is an episode in the career of a larger-than-life sports superstar, notorious for boozing, brawling and womanising. He is Kevin Butty Sowerbutts, the hero of a raunchy new novel set during an overseas England cricket tour. But fact and fiction soon become blurred. For Butty's outrageous antics have a familiar ring – and that is no surprise considering the book's author is Ian 'Beefy' Botham
*News of the World, September*

Kevin Sowerbutts of Huddersfield disappeared in a puff of smoke and Butty the Bum fancier materialised in his place. He had never seen so many pert posteriors waggling about in British Airways skirts. It was a riveting spectator sport.
*Extract from ITB's novel, Deep Cover, about a scandal-riven cricket tour*

# 1980-1981

## THE GREATEST ALL-ROUNDER?

### The Case For

Batting, Bowling, Fielding

### The Case Against

Batting, Bowling, Captaincy

EVER SINCE ITB EXPLODED ONTO THE TEST SCENE IN THE mid-seventies, it has been argued that he deserves a place among the game's greatest all-rounders. Some even claim that he was the greatest of them all, perhaps the greatest cricketer to have ever lived. But there are others who argue that ITB's early success was based on playing teams weakened by defections to Kerry Packer's cricket circus and that, from 1986 onwards, ITB's skills had declined to the extent that he was not even worth a place in the England side. Never can opinion on such a successful cricketer's skills have been so sharply divided.

Garry Sobers was my one cricket hero. I wanted to be the next Garry Sobers.
*ITB*

## THE CASE FOR...

What Maurice Tate had in common with Ian was a terrific physical build, this great big bottom and the will to fire the ball into the pitch. As batsmen they

were pretty much alike too, although Maurice was clumsier. He was a prodigious straight driver of the ball and a fine cover driver. But he couldn't hook like Ian.
*John Arlott*

I have seen only one person to compare with Botham and that is Garry Sobers.
*Ken Barrington*

Ian Botham could never have seen Keith Miller play but there are great similarities in their cricket.
*Richie Benaud*

In his 25 Tests, from his debut against Australia in 1977 to the India Golden Jubilee Test in 1980, Botham's part in the fall of rival wickets reads like this: wickets 139, catches 36, run-outs 3. In that period, a total of 393 enemy wickets fell to England. By my reckoning, this means Botham had a hand in 45.29 per cent of the rival Test wickets that fell.
*Dudley Doust*

It's impossible to be as good with the ball as you are with the bat. There's only one real exception: Botham.
*Mark Ealham*

Mike Procter, Imran Khan or Kapil Dev. I'm tempted to think again of the first of those, but the overpower-ing choice above either of these has to be Ian Botham, a much better bat than the others and, at his peak in

the late seventies and early-to-mid eighties, totally irresistible as a bowler.
*Graham Gooch selects the finest all-rounder he has played with or against*

He picks up a game by the scruff of the neck and throws it out of the window.
*David Gower*

## ITB'S VIEW

Yeah.
*ITB asked (in 1986) whether he was the world's greatest all-rounder*

I am a bit of a perfectionist.

Ninety-nine per cent of cricket manuals belong in the dustbin.
*ITB's introduction to his own instruction book, On Cricket*

In my life I think I've only had about six hours coaching and the only ones I've listened to have been Tom Cartwright, Kenny Barrington and Viv Richards.

## BATTING

The basic positions he gets into are all orthodox, and the position he takes up for the front-foot drive is wonderful. He puts his front shoulder to the ball, not worrying about the feet, because he knows that the head and feet follow automatically if the shoulder is leading properly. His backlift is excellent, the bat

comes down vertically, the head remains perfectly still and he generates enormous power from that uninhibited follow-through as his throws his arms in the sky.
*Then director of coaching at the National Cricket Association Keith Andrew*

The great thing about Botham is that whenever he picks up his bat he picks it up straight, vertically, with the tip of his bat directly above his hands. His hands are cocked, loaded and ready to go. He's ready to hit every ball. I've looked long enough at lots of good players to realise that anyone who picks up his bat this way gets good timing. It's the difference between an ordinary and a great batsman.
*Ted Dexter*

Botham's enemies have often referred to him as an uncultured slogger and for most ordinary mortals to hit the ball as hard as he does slogging is their only resort. But Botham is not like that. He has always been a very technically correct player and it says chapters for the man that he can still play by the text book while hitting the ball at an enormous velocity.
*Graham Dilley*

We chatted jovially about Botham's left-handed sweep, which Doshi said he [ITB] could play off any ball at any time. Dilip said he liked the shot and that Botham was a genius.
*Peter Roebuck talks to Indian left-arm spinner Dilip Doshi*

Bowling at Botham brings the best from me. I love it.
I've got him out a few times and he has now reached
the stage when he doesn't really want to get out to me
again. If he takes it into his mind to have a slog he is a
good enough player, because he's so correct technically, to get away with it. And on those occasions I
would assume that he is impossible to bowl to.
*Phil Edmonds*

Botham turned in one of his famous innings of
muscular magnificence, taking 184 minutes for his
228. The author found himself complimenting
groundstaff and other doting spectators in retrieving
the ball from distant car parks and the groundsman's
cabbage patch. Some of the sixes reached the Tone and
floated downstream with the fish, for ever out of sight
if not mind.
*David Foot on ITB at Worcester in 1980*

No-one – Jessop, Macartney, Bonnor – could have
treated Test bowling with greater disdain.
*David Frith*

Another possible bonus of Ian going in first in the
World Cup was that a number of the matches were
played in New Zealand, in the All Blacks rugby
stadium, ringed by concrete terracing like our old
soccer grounds. I had noticed how a well struck
boundary had the cricket ball rebounding sometimes
from the concrete right back to the middle – which
did the ball plenty of harm.
*Graham Gooch*

He always keeps his head so still and his eyes level.
Most batsmen defend against the good length ball –
Ian blasts it with great power. If I wasn't a player, I'd
queue to watch him bat ahead of anyone else. He is
quite the longest hitter I've seen and, to my mind, the
complete model for an attacking, dominant batsman.
More so even than Viv [ Richards] – because Both is
very orthodox, 90 per cent of his shots are precisely
correct.
*David Graveney*

It was an enormous blow, it would have been six at
either Taunton or Lord's.
*Richard Hibbit, ITB's games master on the ten year-old's
batting prowess*

Now he's playing so straight and hitting it so far that
fielding tactics are almost irrelevant. He is a unique
cricketer.
*Geoff Howarth in 1983*

Botham, not the bowling, got himself out. I insist on
this because I see no bowling which can embarrass
Botham if he is prepared to take charge.
*CLR James*

I believe Botham to be the hardest hitter of any Test
batsman, or for that matter of any Test cricketer at all.
*CLR James*

Botham had been converted most successfully by

Worcestershire into an opening batsman in limited-
overs cricket and he and Curtis blended into an ideal
partnership. It is something of a mystery why Botham
had never been pushed up the order in one-day
matches earlier in his career. It seems such a waste to
have one of the world's most gifted attacking batsmen
coming in with only a handful of overs remaining
when he is capable of turning the course of a game.
*David Lemmon*

I love the way he picks the bat up from the gully area
with such a flourish that helps him to play inside-out,
and so hit sixes over extra-cover. He is truly an
amazing player.
*Ken McEwan*

You can't do much about Both when he's in that kind
of mood. The only way to be certain of getting him
caught is to have two fielders standing in the crowd
100 yards behind the bowler.
*Clive Rice after ITB had scored 90 in 77 balls against Notts*

By Wednesday evening Ian Botham had scored 473
runs off 345 deliveries bowled to him in first class
matches this season. At the crease he has been a
storm, a violent, rolling thunder. His runs have been
scored, not with the flashing hits of Jessop but with
the authority of a Hammond. This spring he has
played his shots better than at any time in his career,
especially the on-drive which he had never previously
mastered. Botham is a superb backplayer – pulling,

driving, hooking – and has a fierce off drive. But his legside strokes have tended to angle square of the wicket. This season they have been thumping through mid-on.
*Peter Roebuck in 1985*

Ian Botham nearly killed me! Not with fist or car either, but with a cricket ball. I was perched on the little white boundary wall with Malcolm Nash at long off in front of me. Botham went after one of the Glamorgan bowlers and hit a very high shot. It was going to be a catch. However, neither Nash nor I had ever seen a ball which accelerated faster than gravity on its downward path. This did. Nashie dived one way, I went the other, and the ball knocked a chunk of masonry out of the wall where I was sitting. Fifteen years later, the mark is sill there.
*Jan Studts*

## ITB'S VIEW

Concentrate, keep your head still and get it over the ball, get behind the line, get your foot to the ball when you play forward, bring the bat through straight, extend the arms when you play shots.
*ITB's six batting principles*

## BOWLING

His hand action is excellent, he thinks people out with variations and he has the courage to try out experiments. Since his injuries I've been even more impressed as he's cut down his pace and seamed it

around as well as swinging it. I've talked bowling with him in depth and found his ideas fascinating.
*Jack Bannister*

I think Botham worked a lot of time on the batsman getting too confident. Instead of bowling to a batsman's weaknesses, a lot of time I think Both used to bowl to your strength. Okay, you might hit him for a couple of fours, but he sets a field so that if you muck that shot up you're going to get out.
*David Boon*

His greatest asset is the ability to swing the ball sharply at pace, especially away from the right-hander but also, with occasional great effect, inwards. The swinging yorker has at times been as close to unplayable as any delivery can be. He also bowls an outrageous slower ball – perhaps the slowest I have seen from a bowler of his normal pace.
*Mike Brearley*

I can't think of a bowler in the world who uses the crease as much as Ian does. When he runs in at you, you have no indication which way he will swerve – if he swerves at all. He doesn't observe the norms of a seam bowler. When a seam bowler goes wide of the crease, you can normally expect an in-swinger, but from out there Ian is just as likely to bowl an out-swinger.
*Sunil Gavaskar*

How many times has he bowled crap, come off at 0 for 60 and ended up with 6 for 90? Perhaps it's because Beefy wouldn't tense up, he'd relax, enjoy himself, banter with the fielders or give a lucky batsman a mouthful.
*Mike Hendrick*

It was typical of Ian. He can bowl you four bad balls in an over and then two magic balls. This one was both.
*Geoff Howarth describes the leg-side long-hop which dismissed him for 94 at Headingley in 1978*

His bowling seems to have an almost hypnotic effect on opponents, trapping them with ordinary balls, enticing miss-hits. He will bowl at anyone, knowing that they are likely to be far more nervous than he is. His growling lbw appeal – a mixture of aggression and slight surprise – has won over many a wavering umpire.
*Simon Hughes*

Yes he did bowl a lot of half-volleys, but they always swung and a wide half-volley that swings gets batsmen out if they go for the drive and don't get over the ball.
*John Lever*

Botham shares with Trueman the ability to make a batsman think he is doing something extraordinary when often he isn't.
*Sir Garry Sobers*

Wickets came Botham's way not merely because he was aggressive, imaginative and at times fast, but also because he possessed the innate facility, given to only a few fast bowlers such as Dennis Lillee, Ray Lindwall and Freddie Trueman, of instinctively pin-pointing an opponent's Achilles heel and tailoring his method of attack accordingly.
*Frank Tyson*

I never had a problem with Ian. For a big man, he ran up very gently and his legs were like iron, which protected his lower back. Both was exceptionally strong, in the same vein as Merv Hughes. He doesn't look fit, but he would bowl all day.
*Somerset and West Indies physio Dennis Waight*

## ITB'S VIEW

It is not so much psychology, as more respect you have earned from past performances, I suppose. Probably the same as when bowlers see Viv walk in.
*ITB on his 'psychological dismissals' with 'bad' deliveries.*

It was wasted on Thommo. It started leg-stump, it held its own for a time so that any batsman would've been into his shot and then it went late and picked out the off-stump. I honestly think it would've beaten any batsman in the world, and Thommo missed it by the width of three bats.
*ITB on a delivery in the 1977 Headingley Test which he regards as the finest he ever bowled*

They're boring.
*Asked why he didn't gain any satisfaction from*
*bowling maidens*

## FIELDING

Ian Botham's extraordinary position close in at second
or third slip was all very well on a dead slow pitch,
but in normal conditions his presence so near their
line of vision must distract the other slip fielders, and
too many of the chances that will come his way will
give him too little time to react. Nevertheless, I prefer
Botham's gambling to the safety-first attitude of many
slip fielders, who stand too deep so as to avoid
dropping catches.
*Mike Brearley*

He is as good an all-round fielder as I've come across.
*Mike Brearley*

Nobody excelled more than Botham, who shrugged
off the discomfort of a twisted left knee to take a
couple of slip catches that were not so much athletic
as a snook at Isaac Newton.
*Rob Steen on ITB's slip-catching during the 1985 Oval Test*
*against the Aussies*

I leave my hands on my knees. Partly this is
arrogance, partly simply tempting fate and partly
because it's a reasonable place to put them. You've no
idea where the catch is coming from, it could be low,
could be wide. Might as well relax until you see it.
*ITB*

63.32 metres
*The distance a 13 year-old ITB threw a cricket ball*

## THE CASE AGAINST...

I thought he was a good cricketer, nothing special.
*Ian Chappell*

He has never fulfilled his potential.
*Imran Khan*

This fellow is the most over-rated player I've seen. He looks too heavy and the way he's been bowling he wouldn't burst a paper bag. I know he's got lots of runs in his career but, from what I've seen, he bats like I used to. The only difference is that I went in at number 10.
*Former Bodyline-bowler Harold Larwood in 1983*

I don't think you could rank him with the all-time greats.
*Alan McGilvray*

It's the greatest load of tommyrot I have ever heard.
*Bill O'Reilly on the claim that ITB was the century's greatest cricketer*

I do not think he was a great player. A very good player, yes, who could have been a great one. But he didn't. He paid little attention to his fitness. If the true test of a top class cricketer is how he performs under pressure against the strongest opposition, then Ian

was found wanting. Sir Richard Hadlee is the all-rounder I most admire.
*Sir Garry Sobers*

## BATTING

A lot of Ian's batting is preconceived. If he thinks I am going to toss it up, he will go for it, whether I toss it up or not. Sometimes he will get away with this and sometimes he won't. But at the end of the day the percentages will be against him.
*Bishen Bedi*

He think's he's a good hooker but he's not. He puts it in the air, he's a compulsive hooker. He should learn to duck under them, because he has so many other shots he doesn't need to hook.
*Keith Fletcher*

I don't think he relishes the real bouncer as much as he thinks he does.
*Geoff Lawson*

Botham and Javed Miandad are batsmen who have to dominate their opposition mentally and tactically if they are to score runs. This is almost impossible to do against the Windies pace quartet, such is their skill and, particularly, because of the small number of deliveries from which it is possible to score. This soon frustrates players like Botham and Miandad, for whom an inability to keep their score moving is almost an affront to their manhood.
*Michele Savidge and Alastair McLellan*

He couldn't bat to save himself.
*Jeff Thomson in 1980*

## BOWLING

His in-swinger is not all that accurate. I don't think his bouncer is a wicket-taking ball. It is not quick enough and it bounces in his half of the wicket, so you can see it coming. Ian bowls a lot of rubbish that goes unpunished.
*Bishen Bedi*

Don't associate me with him. He's overrated. Botham only did well because all the best players had joined Packer. I'd love to have faced him.
*Denis Compton*

Being overweight at best betrays a character weakness, at worst a dereliction of duty. In a highly paid professional sportsman it is hard to forgive, although it clearly suited Botham's psyche to be beefy. There were times nonetheless when he was quite fat. This decreased his mobility as well as contributing to the back problems which took much of the sting out of his bowling.
*Tony Francis*

I've got to say it gave me immense pleasure to pass him in India in 1988 as Test cricket's leading wicket taker. It always rankled me that Botham was the world record-holder because, frankly, I don't rate him as a bowler these days.
*Richard Hadlee in 1989*

The team has been consistently unbalanced because of the decline in Botham's bowling. He should not have been given the new ball during this period [1982-84], but he frequently was and his wayward length, both with new ball and old, too often gave the batsman the chance to hit the boundary which brings confidence.
*Christopher Martin-Jenkins*

Sustained by popular affection and his status as a superstar, and invariably able to reassert himself with consistent batting and fielding contributions, Botham perhaps too belatedly examined his bowling returns. It can be argued that he persisted with ultra aggressive, strike-bowling methods even when, manifestly, they were not bringing the rewards they hitherto offered. While batting genius can be maintained almost intuitively, few bowlers will gain continuing success if they fail to think about the game.
*Neville Scott and Nick Cook*

He paid little heed to fitness, which meant his back suffered further undue strain and he was unable to move the ball away from the right-hander once he started to put weight on in his late twenties.
*Sir Garry Sobers*

He couldn't bowl a hoop downhill.
*Fred Trueman in 1985*

## CAPTAINCY

Garry Sobers, the finest all-rounder in the history of the game, could not successfully nor happily incorpo-

rate the captaincy into his normal round of batting, bowling and close fielding. Neither, as it proved, could Botham.
*John Arlott*

His main problem was that he has been too sensitive to criticism. He allowed people to niggle and upset him.
*Mike Brearley*

The trouble for Botham begun when Hendrick declined to make the tour [to the West Indies]. Many believed that the Derbyshire bowler was unwilling to to serve any longer under Botham. The England captain's dictatorial and tactless attitude has certainly lost him some friends. As a strategist he was weak and he had earned the reputation of being non-appreciative and having favourites. Above all he tried to take too much on himself at a time when his own ability was in question.
*Pelham Cricket Year, 1981*

Botham undoubtedly had a very good cricket brain to accompany his vast natural ability, but was arguably far better suited to the role of vice-captain. Periodically, he could offer a valuable idea to the bowler or captain and express his thoughts well, but the requirement to concentrate his mind at all times tended to stifle a feel for the game which, to his later detriment sometimes, was largely instinctive. His thought process dealt more in flashes of incisive

understanding than in constant analysis. Botham could produce such astonishing feats precisely because he was the perfect natural cricketer. To demand that in addition he should keep a methodical or contemplative eye on events was effectively to deprive him of his unique strengths.
*Neville Scott and Nick Cook*

Botham's virtues as a cricketer did not extend to a gift for leadership which moreover took almost all the flair and effectiveness from his own play.
*EW Swanton*

When he suddenly had to start organising and putting the team to together, he couldn't do it.
*Fred Trueman*

# HERO

Botham has helped to restore cricket to its true glory. After the locust years of dreadful caution and dire mediocrity, heroes are now with us again and nobleness walks, if not 'in our ways,' at least in our cricket fields again.
*Michael Croft, Director of the National Youth Theatre*

I'll never believe you mustn't carry the fight to the enemy. And I'll go on believing that till the day I die.
*ITB*

If I'd been in the war, I'd have won the VC – but it would've been posthumous.
*ITB*

Iron Bottom, Iron Bottom, I love you, I love you.
*Somewhat over-excited Indian fan during the 1981-82 tour*

Botham is the only one I would rush like mad down to the ground to watch if I heard he was 20 not out.
*David Acfield*

If you made him Prime Minister tomorrow, he'd pick
this country up in ten minutes.
*Bill Alley*

On his good days, and there are many, he bats like
every boy and man in the land dreams of doing.
*Keith Andrew*

No one has ever reacted more gigantically to the
challenge of a match. Perhaps he has batted or bowled
in pedestrian fashion, but if so he has not noticed it;
and neither have the spectators. Ian Botham, is above
all, in our day, the man to watch.
*John Arlott*

He was so competitive on the field but regardless of
how he performed he was the first person in your
dressing room afterwards. Not many people can do
that, me included, if you have had a bad day.
*Allan Border*

They, of all people, spend so much time knocking Ian,
yet the man is a national hero. The comments made
me fume. It's almost as if Trueman never bowled a
bad ball, or Compton and Dexter didn't play a bad
shot in their whole careers. [If you don't want
Botham] then we'll take take him off your hands with
pleasure. If Botham was wearing the green cap, there
would not be a shadow of doubt about which side
would win the Ashes.
*Allan Border takes the extraordinary step of holding a press*

*conference during the 1985 Ashes series to defend ITB
against attacks made by former players. Compton, in
particular had accused ITB of 'thinking himself bigger than
the game'*

Almost seventy years ago my father wrote a letter to
*The Times*, saying that no game which did not require
pluck and physical courage could be called 'great'. I
wonder how many people, like myself, notice how Ian
Botham goes to the wicket wearing nothing more
round his head than his beard, whereas other less
exciting and magical batsmen appear looking like a
motor-scooter windshield with transistor earphones.
Perhaps there is a lesson here somewhere?
*Newsreader Reggie Bosanquet, father of BJT Bosanquet
inventor of the googly*

The attack [on ITB] has been spearheaded by the
Right Wing media – backed up by former cricketers
with Right Wing backgrounds – Compton,
Illingworth. Why? Botham is a working-class hero. He
comes form the same social background as the
'impressionable youth' who watch him.
*Robert Boswell (after ITB had been banned from first-class
cricket for smoking pot)*

Ian Botham put a fatherly paw on my shoulder and
said: 'Just stay at the wicket, Fiery, it'll come'.
*The 38 year-old Geoff Boycott receives some advice from the
23 year-old ITB on the 1978-79 tour of Australia*

If I went blind tomorrow, I could happily sustain

myself into old age, by calling into my mind's eye the images which that earth-shattering summer emblazoned for ever on my subconscious.
*E J Brack remembers 1981*

He has a rare generosity to those of less ability; he values the stodgy but resolute contribution of a hard-working batsman and a word of acknowledgment from him means more than fulsome praise from others.
*Mike Brearley*

We live in an era of cost-effectiveness, though occasionally a giant like Botham transcends all calculation.
*Mike Brearley*

Only trying to bat like my idol.
*Surrey batsman Alistair Brown reacts to ITB's allegations that he was a slogger*

It was the last over before tea and he played three defensive shots in a row. I taunted him down the wicket – 'Both, you're not playing for tea, are you?' Next ball he rushed down the wicket and was stumped by yards. He said nothing to me. But he smiled that big smile ...'
*Nick Cook, after ITB had hit the Leicestershire attack for 47 off 51 balls*

His presence at Worcester between 1987 and 1991 transformed a team full of bad haircuts into a team

full of bad haircuts that won trophies.
*Matt Cooper*

I really love the bloke. Both's everything I always
wanted to be as a cricketer. He's never had any fear
and that's how I try and go about my cricket.
*Dominic Cork*

For anyone who can remember the summer of '81,
there is the knowledge, the certainty, that no cause is
ever lost.
*Philip Cornwall*

It was a great experience to bowl to him. We are just
like the crowd when he comes on to the field; there's a
little buzz among us fielders.
*Glamorgan's John Derrick*

He's fat, he's round, he hits 'em out the ground.
*Durham fans greet another ITB six*

I told Ian, 'Just concentrate on your cricket. The
people will come through the turnstiles. The people
love you. They love what you do for cricket'.
*Elton John*

Botham's policy at Dunkirk would have been to try
and march on Berlin.
*Matthew Engel*

The sheer precocity of Botham was a large part of his

appeal. He went for his shots, he lived dangerously. His cricket was often naive, or defiant. He dominated whole columns of the record books. But, like all men of instinct, the pattern would inevitably be inconstant.
*David Foot*

The only thing I've had to do with Both over the years is earn his respect, because he's a great player and great players don't give it away.
*Mike Gatting*

I'm not the type to follow a match through the day, once I'm out. But whenever Botham batted I'd be out there watching. He always made something happen.
*Graham Gooch*

I have witnessed him slip a £10 note into the unsuspecting pocket of an old man down on his luck.
*Frank Hayes*

If we had a corner kick, for example, Ian would carefully position himself outside the penalty area and once he got the ball, he would head it down neatly, then kick a cannon ball into the net. From about 20 yards, too.
*Richard Hibbit, ITB's games master on the nine year-old ITB*

He was excessive – but Regency England would have recognised him instantly. For Ian Botham, read John Bull.
*Derek Hodgson*

He's Biggles, Raffles and Errol Flynn all rolled into one. And I'm going to take him to Hollywood and get him in the movies. He's England's answer to Tom Selleck.
*Tim Hudson*

[These negative aspects] were far outweighed by the positive; the invigorating confidence his name on the scoreboard generates in the team, the inhibitions it instils in the opposition (how many times did he receive a juicy four-ball having just taken guard?), the power, the dominance, the 'watch-out!' swagger.
*Simon Hughes*

He is still an awesome opponent. His skill is in his eyes, which remain razor sharp and sanction reflexes of astonishing speed, and in his hulking shoulders ever able to propel awkward bouncers to the unsuspecting or launch the bat in that distinctive wide arc. He is like the ageing cat that can still pounce and grab the errant mouse.
*Simon Hughes in 1992*

England never adequately replaced Botham and those of us privileged to watch cricket while he was playing can state with some conviction that they never will.
*Martin Johnson*

My father was dying of cancer in the Royal Free Hospital at Hampstead. It was a lingering horrible death that took five months. Ian and I were due for

one of our regular drinking sessions and I rang him to call it off, explaining about my father. 'Where is he'?, he asked. We got a cab to the hospital and he sat there with Dad for half-an-hour. Dad died six weeks later. Believe me, he wasn't worried anymore about death. Ian had made him happy.
*Former Lord's ground staff head boy Bill Jones*

John Lennon declared 'A working class hero is something to be'. Botham rampagingly made flesh of the lyric.
*Frank Keating*

On the cricket field, we would not forget him if we could (and could not forget if we would), as morning after morning the summer's sun rose for him and he went forth and trod fresh grass – and the expectant, eager cry was sent about the land. 'Botham's In'.
*Frank Keating on ITB in the summer of 1985*

The nation stops when Botham goes into bat.
*Frank Keating*

He should be paid for bringing the game into repute.
*Frank Keating, when asked on BBC2's Newsnight how ITB should be treated in the light of his admission to having smoked pot*

He is a walking saint.
*Gary Lineker on ITB's charity walks*

On the one hand, we had Botham's particularly muscular style of smashing balls for six at grounds all over the world; on the other, every Tuesday and Thursday during the same years, we saw Thatcher baiting, hectoring and ruthlessly savaging Neil Kinnock. You didn't have to like Botham or Thatcher to admire the raw energy of their attack.
*Jonathan Margolis*

After a Somerset match at which Headingley spectators abused Viv Richards. Ian Botham called them 'racial idiots'. The Yorkshire Committee had the nerve to demand an apology.
*Mike Marqusee*

Botham, when batting or bowling, even when fielding in the slips, is capable of spreading an excitement that makes fans of people who would normally subscribe to the crude prejudice than cricket is only slightly less boring than watching celery grow or car bumpers rust.
*Hugh McIlvanney*

Botham is devoid of any sense of physical danger and would rather die than display fear.
*Don Mosey*

Gavaskar considers Ian Botham to be England's great-est all rounder. His ability to stir the crowd, his efficient and smooth captaincy and the modesty with which he enjoyed fame and success are the distinctive

features which he respects and espouses.
*Clifford Narinesingh*

He is a great man.
*Douglas Osborne, administrator of the Leukemia Research Fund*

My first impression of Botham was that he was not that much to look at. But he was a mover! He had neither the physique nor the suppleness of Nureyev but in a straight line he was like a whiteout of an avalanche.
*Ingrid Pitt*

What a pity Ian Botham hasn't been put in charge of the England Test team, whose players have been told to watch what they say. He would welcome free speech, especially if things aren't going right. After all, it is criticism that perfects the endeavour.
*AC Preece, letter to Today, May 1995*

He was not at all like other English cricketers. He did not have a superior air about him. His approach to cricket seemed more West Indian than English. He was a marvelously destructive player, fuelled by pride and courage.
*Viv Richards*

He accepted challenges for the hell of it, for the fun of it. When I played against him at Fenners I waited until he had settled in his stance for his first ball, then

I asked my deep mid-wicket to advance ten yards in
from the boundary. Ian's eye lit up and notions of
playing himself in were immediately scrapped – my
invitation to clear the fielder could not be resisted. He
swung massively, miss-hit and the ball drifted just
over my man to bounce inside the ropes for four. He
guffawed, finding the whole thing hilarious. He
would have laughed if the teasing had succeeded.
*Peter Roebuck*

No one studying him that day could have failed to
grasp his extraordinary powers, for here was a man so
often happy to rejoice in vulgarity, silently picking his
way forwards.
*Peter Roebuck on ITB's match-winning innings in the 1983
B&H semi-final*

He could be outrageous, but it did not worry him. He
never doubted his destiny.
*Peter Roebuck*

That's part of my childhood gone.
*Durham wicket-keeper Chris Scott watches ITB walk off the
field for the last time*

Without the flamboyance and vigour of Lillee and
Thomson, no cricket would have been played on our
school field and the sweet shop robbery rate would
have stayed as it was. No Englishmen could have
inspired us as those Australian's did; until the arrival
of Botham. Suddenly boys everywhere could love the

English game without being thought of as weird.
Instead of an image of stripey ties and poems about
WG Grace, cricket was a game of excitement, tension,
fear, audacity, guile, patience and passion.
*Mark Steel*

Ian Botham is Britain's biggest hero since Nelson –
and that includes Churchill.
*The Sun*

On first impressions, I quite like Ian Botham. He
walks Lakeland mountains, and I know that if I were
lost in foul weather on Helvellyn and he appeared out
of the rain and mist, I would feel instantly certain of
my safe homecoming; he has that sort of leadership
and presence.
*Sunday Telegraph*

Ian Botham has many spectacular achievements to his
name, but it's possible that his most outstanding
contribution was to ensure the continued popularity
of 'official' Tests.
*Allen Synge*

He must have put more backsides on seats than any
other English cricketer since Denis Compton.
*Bob Taylor*

I learn from a poll commissioned by Polaroid that Ian
Botham is the 27th most stylish person in Britain.
Only one other sportsman got into the top 5 –

Sebastian Coe, at 43rd. Fascinating to recount, 60% of Botham's votes came from men under 35, while Coe's support came mainly from over-45s.
*The Times*

Everything is just much more interesting when Beefy's around. There is no normality, no groove. He breaks all the rules, so planning against him is pretty impossible. Sometimes, when he bats, I hope and pray that he is going to get out early – but there is a sneaking little feeling at the back of my brain that keeps saying, 'Okay, he's in the mood, why not settle back and enjoy it.'
*Jeff Thomson*

Ian Botham was the strongman of the modern game, the messianic Hercules of English cricket. Everything about him was robustly larger than life, from his brawny physique to his overpowering presence both on and off the field. Before he took over the reins of captaincy, he frequently and presumptuously assumed the role of leader and was often seen directing traffic in the field like an unofficial off-duty policeman. Ian loved and admired power. He worshipped strength in those around him, and even gave grudging admiration to those who were strongly but honestly antagonistic to his behaviour, calling them 'gorillas'.
*Frank Tyson*

No number of dossiers on the opposition, fielding

charts, training routines and fitness assessments can be a replacement for talent. The 'Champagne boys' (Botham, Lamb and Gower) were simply the best players and Mickey Stewart's reign as England manager will be remembered for not producing one player who seriously and genuinely challenged this trio.
*Bob Willis*

The greatest advertisement this game has ever had.
*Bob Willis*

Ian stood by me, kept me in his side longer than I deserved and never stopped encouraging. I remember too his staunch friendship and support. Both refused to let me give in, cajoling me to keep trying.
*Bob Willis on ITB's captaincy*

Ian Botham is a determined, straightforward, pleasant character, who knows where he is aiming, and who, in the best old fashioned sense, has 'a good conceit of himself'.
*1978 Wisden Almanack*

Botham has performed such deeds as have lifted the heart of a nation, and it can have been possible to say that of very few cricketers.
*John Woodcock*

Just as Jimmy Page, Led Zep's guitarist, could lead his band down heavy rock roads or up quiet stairways, so Botham possessed the technical ability and the temperament to play as a situation demanded.
*Graeme Wright*

BOY'S TOP TWENTY HEROES
The men whose work they most like.
1. Eddie Murphy
2. Richard Branson
3. Jasper Carrott
4. Daley Thompson
5. Steve Davis
6. Noel Edmonds
7. David Attenborough
8. IAN BOTHAM
9. Jim Bergerac
10. Sebastian Coe

The men they would most like to be.
1. Daley Thompson
2. Eddie Murphy
3. Richard Branson
4. Jasper Carrott
5. Steve Davis
6. IAN BOTHAM
7. Jim Bergerac
8. Noel Edmonds
9. Sebastian Coe
10. Kenny Everett
Survey by Barclays Bank, 1988

SPORTS PERSONALITY OF THE CENTURY
1. IAN BOTHAM
2. Bobby Moore
3. Stanley Matthews
4. Lester Pigott

5. Douglas Jardine
6. Bobby Charlton
7. Linford Christie
8. W.G. Grace
9. Gordon Banks
Competition organised by The Observer, 1995

'Have you faced a West Indian at 100mph? No. Well I rest my case. It's a life threatening situation. People have been killed playing cricket. I've had my whole face caved in. I've metal here, a crowbar to bring my cheeks out. You think about it, 6oz of leather hitting you at 90mph. It bloody hurts. It breaks arms, skulls, legs. Your hands get mutilated, smashed to pieces.' He thrusts his hands across the table, and sure enough, they are a sorry sight. So crippled he can barely place his palms flat. 'They have been broken two or three times and because you are a professional, you take the injection and go out and play with them broken. I've a muscle between my ribs that I damaged in 1986. The normal recovery time for that injury would be eight to 12 weeks. I was playing four weeks later. Now I suffer every day with that injury, and I will for the rest of my life. I was on anti-inflamatories every day for seven years. And that is not good for you. The body is only just recovering. It's nice in the morning to get out of bed without a routine to get everything going. I can almost get up like a normal person now.'
*ITB talks to Today's Catherine O'Brien*

# VILLAIN

Temperament
Bigmouth Strikes Again
Behaviour
Dedication

Walk into any bad pub in Britain and you will see a dozen young men looking like Ian Botham. Gathered near the jukebox and the pool table they will be looking either bored or angry. They won't laugh unless someone breaks something or hits somebody. I would not go so far as to say that they all model themselves on our fading cricketing genius – it could be the other way around. All I know is that Botham embodies the yobbishness of the Eighties as perfectly as WG Grace stood for the solidity of the Edwardian era.
*Charles Moore, editor, The Spectator, 1988*

His life in cricket has never been comfortable – and he has only himself to blame for much of the trouble he's been in.
*Richard Hadlee*

## TEMPERAMENT

Perversely, as his bowling powers waned from 1980 onwards, so his insistence on hogging the bowling increased, until it is not overstating the case to say

that his reluctance to let other people bowl has contributed towards more defeats than wins or even draws.
*Jack Bannister*

He captains the side like a great big baby.
*Henry Blofeld in 1980*

I told him in 1981 that he should not have been given the captaincy until he was 31 or 32, because I could not see him growing up before then.
*Geoff Boycott*

Botham would, in the later overs of a one-day match when he might be fielding near the boundary, edge around the fence trying to pick out anyone who was harassing him.
*Mike Brearley*

People are getting tired of the petulance and histrionic behaviour of some players. This disgraceful behaviour by Botham brings shame on the good name of sports-men and cricket. It sets a terrible example to the crowd and could be a contributory factor to crowd misbehaviour.
*John Carlisle MP gets on his high horse about ITB's run in with umpire Alan Whitehead during the 1985 Ashes Series*

It was during the Second Test at Barbados. Holding was bowling very well and Botham just couldn't get his bat anywhere near the ball. Once he just threw the

bat on the floor as if to say 'I can't play this stuff'.
Eventually he was out caught behind off Holding for
26 and he comes storming into the dressing room
shouting 'What can you do? You can't do this, you
can't do that.' And there's all us tailenders sitting
there thinking, 'We haven't got half the talent of this
man and he's making a song and dance about not
being able to play the bowling. What chance do we
have?'
*John Emburey on ITB the captain*

On returning from the West Indies tour, Botham
travelled with Somerset for a county championship
game against Lancashire. When he went out to bat,
who should be waiting for him but Lancashire's then
overseas player Michael Holding. Botham told his
partner, opening batsman Peter Roebuck, that he
wouldn't survive the over. He didn't: he was out first
ball, his confidence shot to pieces.
*Michele Savidge and Alastair McLellan*

David Gower will come and have a knock-up because
he's been captain and he knows how important it is
for everyone to join in. Both has a slightly shorter
memory of his captaincy days, when he needed
people to make just a little bit of effort.
*Mike Gatting*

Botham, especially when he was captain, seemed
unable to control his instincts for long enough to be
able to set an example to others.
*Imran Khan*

Judging by his performance in recent years, it seems as though he has not learned much from his experiences or used them to improve his game.
*Imran Khan in 1986*

Botham said to an interviewer that he wanted to captain England again. When the interviewer asked why, Botham replied that he wanted to get back at the critics. I almost wept, for Botham has fine cricketing qualities, but a commonplace mind which cannot organise them.
*CLR James*

Cricketers are nothing if not realists, and Botham's out-of-the-trenches-and-over-the-top leadership has begun to pall when there is a battery as devastating as Holding and company waiting for them.
*Robin Marlar*

For too long Botham failed to come to terms with the fact that the attitude which made him one of the most feared opponents in the game needed to be rethought. Part of the problem here was that other people in positions of influence on the England scene effectively deferred to Botham's own estimate of his strengths. They, too, recalled matches won by inspired bowling performances and unsurprisingly, were reluctant to steer his efforts in a different direction. The effect of such thinking was to delay English cricket's self-examination.
*Neville Scott*

Ian Botham is all mouth
*Jeff Thomson*

There doesn't seem to be a defensive thought in his
head, even at a time when defence is the only sensible
course.
*Bob Willis*

## BIGMOUTH STRIKES AGAIN

Just remember one thing son, you've already been
killed once on a cricket field.
*ITB in 1978 to New Zealand's Ewan Chatfield after he had
run out Derek Randall while the Englishman had been
backing up. Three years earlier, Chatfield had been knocked
unconscious by a bouncer from English fast bowler Peter
Lever. His heart stopped beating and only prompt action by
England physio Bernard Thomas saved his life*

I am very proud of our heritage. Unlike the
Australians at least we have one.
*ITB*

I hope I never have to go Pakistan again. I think it's a
place to send your mother-in-law for a month, all
expenses paid.
*ITB*

I hope John Major knocks Europe for six.
*ITB's contribution to the mad cow debate, June 1996*

I don't ask Kathy to face Mike Holding, so there's no

reason why I should be changing nappies.
*ITB*

No 57, Pilau Rice.
*ITB to the Karachi born Essex batsman Nadeem Shahid
who was busy pasting him around the park*

I would love to sit in a deck chair and watch Malcolm
Marshall knock his head off.
*ITB, asked (in 1989) if he would like to tour the West
Indies with Somerset's Peter Roebuck, the man who had
played a major role in getting his friend Viv Richards
sacked as one of the county's overseas players in 1986*

## BEHAVIOUR

Unfortunately, the subject of the Cider County also led
to a vintage display of oikishness in the form of a
cruel parody of Peter Roebuck. Botham went off into a
flight of fantasy picturing Roebuck opening for
England against the Windies at Sabina Park and
Richards handing the ball to Patterson with the
words, 'I don't like this guy'. Botham preceded to act
out the scene, portraying himself sniggering behind a
newspaper in the dressing room as Roebuck was led
away with a few broken ribs.
*Steve Amos reports on the 'Beefy' Roadshow*

Botham has always had followers; but, the point is, he
did not actually lead them anywhere. It was sufficient
that they adored him. Botham has always been a
creator of courts and he demands not equals but

courtiers.
*Simon Barnes*

It is no use relying on Botham and the like suddenly
realising the error of their ways. They will only do so
when they are past hell-raising and trouble-making
and want to make easy money as consultants,
television show performers and so forth.
*Derek Birley*

If you want to be the best, you have to be bloody
selfish. You also have to have stability. Most top
sportsmen have their mate, someone to go home to,
someone who is not in the game and who will cook
you a meal when you are down. I never took cricket
home, but what I didn't realise was what Kath was
going through. I had the dressing room, my mates to
help me laugh things off, but Kath still had to walk
down to the shops, the kids still had to go to school.
*ITB*

When Ian was captain his stubbornness encountered
dangerously few obstacles. One England player told
me that he was physically afraid to pursue a
suggestion if Ian had once disagreed with it.
*Mike Brearley*

Within 24 hours of public disgrace, Botham was
casting himself in the role of victim. Only an ego
monstrously bloated by persistent adulation and high-
calorie sycophancy could have reached such a conclu-

sion. The sycophancy has hastened his downfall. Wherever Botham goes, there too go willing acolytes ready to clap his back, cackle at his antics and, fatally, stand him a drink.
*Patrick Collins after the ITB's sacking by Queensland*

By your prowess you have earned a large following of thousands of young impressionable people. You may wish to reflect whether, in view of this offence, you have set them the right example.
*Magistrate Gerald Fish admonishes ITB after fining him £100 for possession of Cannabis in 1985*

Botham had already decided to sign with Somerset for one more season instead of two. Then his resignation from the county captaincy was announced in the tabloid, to which he was contracted, before the county were told.
*David Foot*

The glamour stuff didn't suit Taunton. All those television cameras and hordes of reporters packing out a small ground ruined its intimacy for many people and Botham was held responsible for that.
*David Foot*

Ian Botham's motto was 'never come back the day you go out'. I think he tends to be a bit paranoid about people who like to live their life to the full during the daytime, and then enjoy a sound night's kip to prepare for the next day.
*Graham Gooch*

I think people let him get away with too much early in his career because he was such a good player. But now his behaviour is pretty damning and can't go on forever.
*Tom Graveney in 1988*

Botham was cut off in his prime by a breakback from John Stephenson. The dismissal betrayed Botham's irritating side. He complained that he had been distracted by a man flashing a mirror behind the bowler's arm. He was so churlish about it that an official was dispatched to flush out the culprit. In vain, of course: this is County Durham, not Delhi.
*Simon Hughes*

Some younger team mates found his presence rather daunting. This was either because they lacked confidence, or suspected he did not value their ability. Often they were right and their form faded as a result.
*Simon Hughes*

I can remember Ian when he got married and I can't believe it's the same fellow. When I knew him then, he was just a nice, quiet lad and now ...
*Mrs Shirley Illingworth after ITB's constant criticism of her husband Ray, England's chairman of selectors*

Some silly bitches would be delighted to think that I kill just for the sake of killing. I don't. I eat what I kill.
*ITB the hunter*

What neither of us knew was that we were supposed to be limited to one stag each. Both was now shooting like he batted – letting fly at anything that moved, and that's why, instead of two stags, we ended up with four, plus a fox and a grouse.
*Allan Lamb*

If some bloke was asleep in the dressing-room he would set his pants on fire or something, but if he was asleep no-one was allowed to touch him.
*Allan Lamb*

If he hadn't married, I reckon he'd have ended up inside.
*Jim Laws*

[ITB] forgot, or chose to overlook, that Hayter was worth far more to him than the percentage of his earnings he claimed, that Hayter had extricated him from an untold number of scraps and potentially damaging headlines by using his vast army of contacts to persuade and placate.
*Alan Lee on ITB's decision to part with his first agent Reg Hayter*

It is important that the TCCB should not let the matter pass – however maladroit their handling of it has been so far – because there is an increased tendency for Botham to consider that he is free to behave as he pleases. His introduction of friends and children into the team environment and his flamboyant commer-

cially motivated dress are not separately so bad, but
collectively can be divisive. What the TCCB need to
remind him is that without umpires, opponents and
colleagues, his extravagant play has no platform. Most
of his colleagues would agree, even if his captain opts
to give evidence on his behalf.
*Chief Times columnist David Miller on ITB's clash with
umpire Alan Whitehead during the 1985 Ashes series*

Peter May, chairman of selectors, courteously made
himself available for questions while Botham
indulged himself in his usual custom of trying to blast
the ball from the nets into the group of correspon-
dents surrounding the chairman. As always it was a
minor miracle that no-one was seriously injured. To
Botham it was, of course, a huge joke as we ducked
and bobbed and dodged. I often think he must watch
video nasties while eating his Shredded Wheat.
*Don Mosey in 1984.*

No, cards are to be avoided, Botham might join in,
and someone will end up whitewashed, or in the bath,
or both. Of course if Botham is not playing cards he
must be doing something else somewhere else.
Possibly he's thumping someone or putting ice-cubes
in socks.
*Peter Roebuck*

Eight of us played golf on a beautiful course. Chilly
(Chris Old) and I ended up playing with a middle-
aged Irishman named Michael Byrne. After a few

holes Guy [the Gorilla - ITB's nickname] joined us. As usual Guy didn't spare the swear words as we played the course. While I was walking down the fairway I asked Mr Byrne what he did for a living - he answered, 'I'm a Roman Catholic Priest'.
*Bob Taylor*

All over the British Isles men and women are giving their time to keep cricket's soul alive, teaching the rudiments of cricket to children in the hope that they will be imbued with something of the philosophy of the game. That is why they despair when a Botham spits, a Broad stands his ground, a Gatting becomes embroiled with an umpire, or half a dozen Pakistani braves converge on another umpire like apaches in pursuit of Jane Russell.
*Graeme Wright*

## DEDICATION

Sure Both has done his tremendous walk from John O'Groats to Land's End, but that doesn't get you fit for cricket. Cricket requires a very specific form of fitness.
*Phil Edmonds during the 1986 tour of the West Indies*

When it was suggested to him by Ian Botham that dawn jogging was sapping his energy, Gooch snapped back: 'You only know about it cos that's the time I pass you on the way home from a party'.
*Tony Francis*

Definitely the least dedicated [when compared to Imran Khan and Kapil Dev]. Too casual about fitness work and match preparation; he just doesn't work as hard as he ought to and it's that slackness which largely accounts for his downward slide.
*Richard Hadlee in 1989*

The approach of two of the senior players, Graham Gooch and Ian Botham, may have been counter-productive. Both have recently made a lot of money out of cricket and therefore winning this series may not have featured high enough on their lists of priorities.
*Christopher Martin-Jenkins (on the 1986 tour of the West Indies)*

Botham didn't help himself all that much in the 1980 season. He thrives on hard work as a bowler but his back injury and the bad weather gave him little chance to keep his weight down. He should have trained harder and looked after himself a little bit more.
*Mike Procter*

A fat has-been.
*Dermot Reeve's opinion of the ageing Botham in 1990*

If Beefy only half-applied himself to his fitness, he'd leave the other bowlers in the England side for dead.
*Clive Rice in 1987*

Bob Willis had told me that there was one rule for Both and another for the rest of us and I quickly knew

what he meant. When we went on runs Ian would jog round the square while we jogged round the outfield and nobody would ever pick him up on it. He was a law unto himself.
*David Smith*

He had a lot of ability but if he had had a more serious manner rather than a happy-go-lucky approach, he could have achieved more.
*Sir Garry Sobers*

Ian's fat content in relation to his body weight was 22 per cent. About 12 is normal for such a big man.
*England Physio Bernard Thomas in 1980*

One of his longest bowls in the nets was against Elton John at the MCG prior to the WSC finals.
*Stephen Thorpe on ITB's attitude to net practice during the 1986-87 tour of Australia*

Ian has suffered with his back for the past three years and never been entirely free from discomfort. That being the case, the worst trap he could fall into is to carry too much weight, which he undoubtedly has done. Four years ago Mike Brearley and myself warned him that he did not have the secret of eternal youth and that the day would come when some hard graft would be called for to keep fit. However, until it stared him in the face, he would not accept it.
*Bob Willis in 1983*

# THE VERDICT

The Press
Past Players
Opponents
Team-mates
Friends, Family and Others

If prominent British sportsmen were drinks, what would they be? Frank Bruno would be a mug of tea, while Ian Botham would be a six-pack of extra-strong lager: brash, powerful, popular and in thoroughly bad taste.
*Jonathan Margolis*

Botham is basically a person who enjoys the limelight and the notoriety, he has tended to flaunt himself in the belief that he can switch off the spotlight when it suits him. It is a dangerous illusion.
*Geoff Boycott*

He is beyond doubt a cricketing genius – that is the problem really, a genius that found itself in the body of an ordinary, troublesome lad from unremarkable Yeovil.
*Peter Roebuck*

He's been a great asset to cricket. But he's not always been a great asset to Ian Botham.
*Elton John*

## THE PRESS

It's incredible to me. We expect this chap Botham to
work cricketing miracles every day and still behave
like a sombre vegetable.
*John Arlott*

Ever since Botham has been paying the price for those
brief weeks in 1981; perhaps, in a way, we all have ...
but, by God, it was worth it.
*Simon Barnes*

Sport and pop music are both areas characterised by
self-obsession. And both these areas produce that
extraordinary thing, the star. Stars provoke extreme
reactions in their public: adoration and loathing. Boy
George and Ian Botham are stars, both monsters of
self-projection.
*Simon Barnes*

Botham snubbed his nose at Lord's when it suited, but
he is true-blue Establishment, a Thatcher man,
Royalist and a disciplinarian for his children.
*Colin Bateman*

Ian Botham is the best thing to have happened to
English cricket since Ted Dexter. Like Dexter, he plays
the game as excitingly as a West Indian. Unlike Dexter
he has the competitiveness of an Australian.
*E J Brack*

Ian Botham, the man who got lager louts interested in

cricket, resembles not so much a cricketer as a
Scunthorpe United reserves centre forward, which
coincidentally, he was.
*Ray Collins*

Paul Allott is a Botham clone, only slimmer and
brighter. Who isn't?
*Frances Edmonds*

You would have to pay me a lot more than forty
grand to sleep with him, what a nauseating prospect.
*Frances Edmonds*

'The thing about Ian', a team-mate told me once, 'is
that he believes doing one great thing cancels out all
the shitty ones'.
*Matthew Engel*

It is Botham's destiny never quite to match his mate
Viv no matter how he tries.
*Matthew Engel*

Botham had brought fame and infamy to Somerset.
Often he has looked stronger than the county. But he
has also undeniably loved Somerset. He's highly
marketable, highly quotable and a man of surprising
complexity. He's flawed – and he knows it. The
sweeping paradoxes of his nature will never disap-
pear. He will remain likeable, irritating and contemp-
tuous of many conventional standards.
*David Foot*

Under constant observation from the media, Ian Botham can't keep anything private and his image is already a target for the tabloid scavengers. However, little appears to have been said about a succession of interesting hairstyles that have detracted any street credibility that the great all-rounder might have been endeavouring to accrue, except perhaps in a gathering of designer-clothed First Division soccer players.
*Peter Hardy*

Had he kept his swashbuckling for cricket, he might single-handedly have made the game so attractive that crowds would have been encouraged without the need to dress up players in pyjamas.
*Roy Hattersley*

The critics would do well to answer one question. What would they have been like if they had his gifts, stamina, build, courage and record when 22 years old?
*Eric Hill*

Cricket reflects a man's character like no other sport and had Botham not been larger than life off the field, neither would he have been the player he was on it.
*Martin Johnson*

[Botham's finest moments were] logged with swash and buckle, a wolfish grin and a promise of foaming pints or vintage wines.
*Frank Keating*

To Botham, in his Peter Pan world, it was forever 1981
and the Australians were being slain by his flashing
sword.
*Alan Lee*

The cricket writer has to be as much a sleuth, lawyer
and vicar to asses Ian Botham and think of a
judgment.
*Tony Lewis*

Much of Botham's autobiography has what might be
considered a defensive tone. The tabloid harassment,
the mistakes, the charity walks, the Somerset farrago
and the injuries are often discussed with reference to
'cynics', 'scum' (certain newspaper journos) or people
who don't know 'one end of a cricket bat from the
other'. To the confirmed Botham-hater (and I think
there are more than you might think) this comes
across as mawkish self-justification. To the fan it is
honest and brave.
*Matthew Lloukes*

He has achieved cricketing miracles without having
dedicated himself solely to his profession. As such he
has been a bad example to, and influence on, one or
two young members of the England side who may
have felt that, to 'keep in' with Botham, they had to
behave like him.
*Christopher Martin-Jenkins*

We remember Lloyd George as a Prime Minister, not

as a womaniser; Churchill as a leader and Statesman, not as a father or brandy-drinker; and in time we shall remember Ian Botham as a cricketer.
*Christopher Martin-Jenkins*

Ian Botham puts sport in its place and takes it out of the realm of being a sacrament. In time off he does not deny himself any of the extroversion which 'dedicated' sportsmen are said to eschew. But that does not prevent him from being better than all of them. At the risk of being jailed for treason, I must say that our own great treasure, Don Bradman, was a dreary conservative, who after amassing all those runs, settled in Adelaide as a stockbroker and amassed a great many more dollars than runs. All of his public utterances have been notably conformist.
*James McClelland*

If Botham is an English folk hero, then this must be an alarming time for the nation.
*David Miller*

In so many ways, Ian Botham is a product of modern society with its many imperfections.
*Don Mosey*

As a country we are obsessed by sacrificial victims. Ian Botham, burdened with the sins of English cricket, is much more famous since his fall from grace than ever he was hitting sixes. Indeed, so admirably outlawed has he become, that he is the first cricketer able

to get away with tinting his hair.
*Paul Pickering*

What you have to appreciate about Ian Botham is that
there's an awful lot less than meets the eye. We
analyse him too much and come to conclusions that
aren't even in Botham's vocabulary. He is the ultimate
case of what you see is what you get.
*Ian Stafford*

Seeing a passive Botham is like hearing Paul, George
and Ringo in harness; you can admire the content,
even the sentiments, but it doesn't move you.
*Rob Steen*

His captaincy of England from 1980-81 was not an
unqualified success, and his leadership skills have
often been questioned, but that rather misses the
point. Whatever team Botham is playing in, and
whoever he is playing for, he is always the leader of
the gang.
*The Sunday Times*

Pity the kids who only know him for his self-conscious buffoonery on *A Question Of Sport*. The man
who hasn't got anything better to do with his time
than swap idiocies with David Coleman, was once the
epitome of sporting killer-instinct.
*Paul Thomas*

On and off the field there are no half measures. He
can be both grotesque and charming, irresistibly dash-

ing and utterly boorish.
*John Woodcock*

Left to himself, he looked to be in danger of destroy-
ing his talent, his image and ultimately himself.
*Graeme Wright*

## PAST PLAYERS

I keep telling the blighter that it's only six when he
clears the boundary and it's still six when he clears
the pavilion: he just has to hit the cover off the thing.
*Ken Barrington*

Botham's form slump coincided with his captaincy
stint. This was seized on by many as an excuse that
Botham should not remain as captain of England, but
I wonder what they said after the tour of Australia in
1982-83, where Botham's form, when he wasn't captain, was disappointing. Nothing, I suspect. It was
always a convenient story – that Botham was affected
by the captaincy – but it would have been more
accurate by far to say he was affected by losing.
*Richie Benaud*

He's like a big soft puppy really.
*Tom Cartwright*

The first rock 'n' roll cricketer.
*Len Hutton*

Ian did something for English cricket at a time when it

was in the doldrums, namely bringing people back to the game. Such feats in an era of unprecedented cult status unfortunately blinded others to his failings.
*Sir Garry Sobers*

To appreciate Ian Botham as a sportsman and as an individual, one has to realise that he is the personification of the original Protestant: determined to go to hell in his own way. Although, he could be stubbornly wrongheaded, the Somerset all-rounder never lacked the courage of his opinions – no matter how illogical.
*Frank Tyson*

What happened between his moments of glorious success did not seem to matter. Botham appeared to be driven by an ego-centric fixity of purpose to occupy and dominate centre-stage.
*Frank Tyson*

## OPPONENTS

He's 98 per cent tremendous but he has that streak that makes him go off. I would just like to see him go through a season without major headlines. I'm certain he doesn't help his own cause just by his own nature. Whenever he has a minor hiccup it's an instant paper seller. He has to realise what a big name he is and act accordingly.
*Allan Border*

He is probably the most aggressive player I have seen and I would take some convincing that there has ever

been one with a more competitive nature.
*Greg Chappell*

I get the feeling that Ian is more at ease in the England
side than he is in the Somerset side.
*Greg Chappell*

There is nothing in the world he likes more than to
knock over Australian batsmen or smash our bowlers
around the field.
*Greg Chappell*

Many journalistic briefs comprise, 'eight paragraphs
on why Ian Botham blew the game'.
*Frank Hayes*

People couldn't have it more wrong about Botham
craving attention and Gower being remarkably
discreet: Beefy would like to live in peace and quiet,
go fishing, play with the kids, whereas David can't
live without the limelight.
*Mark Nicholas*

I've often wondered how a great natural cricketer like
Ian Botham managed to slip through the system – it's
refreshing to see an Englishman who attacks with the
bat and crashes the bowlers around when he bats. He
plays like an overseas cricketer: there are mini-
Bothams all over the place in South Africa.
*Mike Procter*

Fleet Street helped to get Ian Botham the England

captain's job by a sustained campaign reminiscent of
the one launched in 1975 to get Tony Greig the job –
the one about the young, dashing all-rounder blowing
the cobwebs away from English cricket by leading
from the front.
*Mike Procter*

## TEAM-MATES

Because he was getting so many runs and knocking
wickets down and because he was such a big fella,
they encouraged him to be stupid. Not just the media,
but the players and the captain as well. It was all
bravado – 'Come on Both, be Guy the Gorilla'.
*Brian Close*

To establish the absolute primacy of Botham, as a
bowler, in England's cricket was an error. From the
period of his greatest triumph, the 1981 series,
Botham's bowling potency, while certainly not
disappearing, greatly declined. To build a side's hopes
around such sharply diminished returns necessarily
invited problems.
*Nick Cook*

Beefy saved all his theories for the golf course. The
one which turned a bad lie into a rabbit scrape and
thence a free drop always seemed a particularly useful
one to me. Cricket on the other hand was all instinct.
*Tim Curtis*

I was reading about tennis player Boris Becker the

other day and how he has made a conscious effort to adjust his life to the demands of fame. But Beefy has never done that. Fame is a double-edged sword, but Botham apparently doesn't see that.
*Phil Edmonds*

It is ridiculous to expect people like Both to play cricket seven days a week and still be fresh enough to win a few Test matches.
*Phil Edmonds*

Left to my own devices, I would never say, 'Come on guys, it's Christmas, let's all dress up!' But Lamby and Both love it. I think that's the case with some people, a kind of enjoying yourself by numbers.
*Phil Edmonds*

Ian paced himself and conserved his energies for the big games and as someone of a similar age I could relate to that, so there were no complaints from me when he missed nets.
*Graham Gooch*

In many ways Ian was a good captain. Tactically he was sound and he was always willing to experiment. As a general team man and inspiration in the dressing-room, captain or not, he was faultless.
*Graham Gooch*

Botham's self belief is such that he could shuffle off to slip with figures of 1-0-36-0 wondering what cruel

hand of fate prevented him from doing the double hat trick.
*David Gower*

He's a million times better bat at 60 for 4 than 300–4.
*David Gower*

He did not spend time analysing a youngster's technique, attitude was far more important. Do you want it, or don't you. If you do, go out and get it; if you don't, on yer bike son. He was frugal with compliments, so they meant more when they were offered.
*Simon Hughes*

The Bothams have the sort of house you might expect. Large, old and next to a pub.
*Simon Hughes*

While he supervised the poaching of wild salmon or the braising of local steak, drinks appeared from all directions. An important by-product of these evenings was to lure leading members of the 'oppo' to excess so they'd be below par next morning. Peter Roebuck noticed a deadly improvement in the Taunton performances of visiting Test stars once Botham had left Somerset.
*Simon Hughes*

Some people would say he was a bully. Everyone was a bit scared of him in the dressing-room. But he was a light-hearted guy, he enjoyed his cricket and that's

why he was so successful.
*Allan Lamb*

He's like my half-brother. There's a lot of love between us.
*Viv Richards*

His instincts are not tamed, his zest for life has not mellowed. His wholeheartedness leads to triumphs and troubles, to success and scrapes, for it is not balanced by a shrewd appreciation of public relations nor by a tolerance of rudeness and criticism.
*Peter Roebuck*

I once told him. 'The thing I most fear about you is your capacity to move whole sections of public opinion behind you'. If Ian took against you, he could do that.
*Peter Roebuck*

It's surprising how much time Botham and Richards spend at the County Ground. They are at the ground much more than other players. Our dressing room is probably the only place apart from their homes where they are not threatened by anyone or anything. It's the only place no-one will be watching them, where their characters are taken for granted and not judged.
*Peter Roebuck*

Botham has no depth of belief in himself. He some-times expresses astonishment that he has taken so

many Test wickets and there are times when even he feels it is not much fun to face a barrage of short balls. After his tour to the West Indies he admitted to being shell-shocked, a concession that Viv Richards would never have made.
*Peter Roebuck*

In some respects Ian and Elton John have much in common. Both have been forced into false, self-absorbed worlds by their success. Botham's room in Epworth is lined with reminders of his triumphs. It is his room, a tribute to himself. At his parties, Elton John entertains his quests by playing his own songs.
*Peter Roebuck*

Never count Both out – of anything.
*Brian Rose*

We're staying at a hotel with a casino, and Both proceeds to lose a hundred dollars in five minutes at roulette. The previous week he won eight dollars at cards, he doesn't seem to care about money, but really loves life.
*Bob Taylor*

You can't expect a man of Ian's talent to be a choirboy.
*Bob Willis*

## FRIENDS, FAMILY AND OTHERS

I suppose I could have married a carpet cleaner. But then it would have been boring, wouldn't it?
*Kathy Botham*

Ian's no saint. Probably at times he's been a bit stupid, but he doesn't deserve the adverse publicity he's got. He's so loyal, very generous, very caring.
*Kathy Botham*

I have this poor little wifey image, but it is not reality. I know my own mind and I have my feet firmly on the ground. Our marriage works well because we are not together all the time. It may sound strange but it is the way it has always been with us. Ian is not an easy person to be around for too long.
*Kathy Botham*

I quite enjoy my independence. When Ian's been home for a few days I am quite glad to see the back of him. He takes up so much time.
*Kathy Botham*

When in doubt, open another bottle of wine.
*(the Botham philosophy)*

We  had organised a foot race, maybe 20 yards, among the children. Ian wasn't much of a sprinter in those days – in fact he was never much of a sprinter – but this time he got out in front and near the finish line he turned round suddenly and bumped down the other children one by one. (ITB was two years old at the time).
*Les Botham (ITB's dad)*

There was a simplicity in Ian [as a child] and it's still there.
*Les Botham*

Ian's favourite pastime once we got to Yeovil was to a throw a hammer through the window. (ITB was now three).
*Marie Botham (ITB's mum)*

He's the only child I've known who used to walk down the street, looking in at all the prams, talking to the babies.
*Marie Botham*

When I was at school I was always being picked on because of Ian's tough-guy image. Even now, I can't drink in my hometown of Yeovil. I go further out, where I am not known. Even girls at school tried to put me down. Often they would ask me out, then after I accepted they would stand me up. The next thing I knew the gossip would be flying around – 'I turned down Ian Botham's little brother'. But I think the world of Ian. He's great company and the rare times we go out for a pint are great.
*Graham Botham (ITB's younger – by ten years – brother)*

I've only known one person like Botham, and that was John Lennon. It's tragic that the 20th century's music phenomenon and modern cricket's most brilliant entertainer never got together. Lennon could go into any room and honestly regard everyone as his equal. It's a priceless ability and it is shared by Beefy.
*Elton John*

I'm not saying Ian is a saint. He's got this image of being aggressive and he's been caught up in many unfortunate things – many of which have been his own fault. His problem is that he rises to the bait in some situations. I often liken him to Sylvester Stallone. They are both forever having to deal with people just dying to have go.
*Elton John*

Some of the older retired England players seem to resent his success. They don't understand the pressure on players these days. Media attention is so intense. Some ex-England cricketers such as Denis Compton, Freddie Trueman and Ray Illingworth come across as very bitter people. I think they're jealous of Ian.
*Elton John*

Ian's so macho, man. When he looks at a girl it's like he's gonna take her. He's got that look that says, 'It's your turn next'. And the women love it.
*Tim Hudson*

There was an element of good fortune about some of those wickets, so I suppose people will say it's typical Botham luck.
*ITB's son Liam Botham, who took 5-67 on his first-class debut in 1996*

You two are nothing but wasters. You'll make nothing of your careers. You'll just drift away. You'll be the people society wants to forget.
*Headmaster to ITB and schoolfriend*

## ITB'S VERDICT

If we're playing some silly game, Liam and I, I can't let him win. It's pathetic. I've even got to beat my one year-old child. (1978)

I will not be playing cricket in ten years time. I won't be involved in the game at all. (1986)

Apart from the Royal family and Mrs Thatcher, I'm probably the most famous person in England. (1986)

The whole object of sport is to have a good time.

I'm still one of the lads, very much so. I will always will be. I still go down the pub with my mates or over the golf course. Because of what I have achieved those mates include Ian Woosnam, Nick Faldo, Colin Montgomery and Elton John. But there's all the local boys too – builders, decorators, firemen. That's the way I've always been. Just Beefy.